Becoming Your Own
Business Coach

Becoming Your Own Business Coach

George W. Watts

PRAEGER

AN IMPRINT OF ABC-CLIO, LLC
Santa Barbara, California • Denver, Colorado • Oxford, England

Library of Congress Cataloging-in-Publication Data
Watts, George W.
  Becoming your own business coach / George W. Watts.
    p. cm.
  Includes bibliographical references and index.
  ISBN 978-0-313-38361-8 (hbk. : alk. paper)—ISBN 978-0-313-38362-5 (ebook)
  1. Executive ability. 2. Executive coaching. I. Title.
  HD38.2.W378 2010
  658.4'07124—dc22   2009048250

ISBN: 978-0-313-38361-8
EISBN: 978-0-313-38362-5

14   13   12   11   10   1   2   3   4   5

This book is also available on the World Wide Web as an eBook.
Visit www.abc-clio.com for details.

Praeger
An Imprint of ABC-CLIO, LLC

ABC-CLIO, LLC
130 Cremona Drive, P.O. Box 1911
Santa Barbara, California 93116-1911

This book is printed on acid-free paper ∞

Manufactured in the United States of America

To my father, George M. Watts

Contents

1

Becoming

The core premise of *Becoming Your Own Business Coach* is straightforward: The deeper and better you understand yourself, the more successful an executive you will become.

In this book, I advocate that reflection, looking within, and analyzing oneself are complementary to—not a substitute for—life experience. Experience by itself is inadequate.

After years of leading as a senior executive, consulting with executives through assessment and testing, and coaching and working closely with hundreds of top performers, CEOs, and successful entrepreneurs, I perceived an underlying attribute many of the most successful seemed to possess.

Outstanding executives or entrepreneurs tend to know themselves very well, including their "shadow" or darker side. They understand their proclivities, weaknesses, and strengths. Whether or not they are likable, most have a pretty clear idea of who they are. They don't sugarcoat their weaknesses or glamorize their strengths. They're able to see and evaluate themselves objectively.

My job is managing partner of AST, a talent management consulting firm. Primarily, our firm does executive assessments; we interview executives for jobs and give in-depth personality, cognitive ability, and aptitude tests. We also coach top performers, give leadership development seminars and retreats, and do extensive organizational development projects.

I have seen aggressive, unlikable people make a lot of money and rise to the top of their organizations. Not that I personally approve of some of their behavior—I don't. However, I've observed that they generally are aware of their temper, stubbornness, abrasiveness, and confrontational personalities. They factor this into their decision making and analysis. These features become part of their company's climate or morale, with associated turnover.

These highly successful people have figured out how to leverage their strengths while managing around their weaknesses. This deeper understanding of "self" is a real differentiator between the people who are stuck in middle management and the people that ascend to, and successfully stay at, senior levels.

This insight of the importance of self-knowledge began to resonate within me to the point where I was inspired to write a down-to-earth, easy-to-read book to help businesspeople gain a greater understanding of who they really are. Much of our executive coaching at AST explores this concept to one degree or another. As I discovered in my doctoral program in counseling psychology, much of what a good counselor does is to help people realize the real reasons behind their actions and behavior.

Becoming Your Own Business Coach is a personal diary of this important self-awareness. My goal for the book is for you to be able to sit down with complete confidentiality—after all, it's only you and the book—and try to get to know yourself a little better on an intimate, friendly level. There is nobody there to judge, nor is there any reason to judge you. This book is just helping you take some "you" time, that's all.

> *Far and away the best prize that life offers is the chance to work hard at work worth doing.*
>
> —Theodore Roosevelt

> *Intelligent people know others. Enlightened people know themselves.*
>
> —Lao Tzu

> *The final mystery is oneself.*
>
> —Oscar Wilde

> *A man should first direct himself in the way he should go. Only then should he instruct others.*
>
> —Buddha

I hope this book inspires you to grow to your potential. Setting high, obtainable goals and believing you have the promise of improvement within you are the two building blocks of your transformation. Suffer no delusions: self-development is hard work. There is a real time investment, effort, and personal commitment needed to analyze oneself, receive feedback openly, and strive for improvement.

How about a little motivation speech? *I believe you have the ability to achieve what your vision of your life is*—to become an admired leader, earn substantial compensation, create an exciting future as an entrepreneur . . . whatever it is that turns you on.

Becoming Your Own Business Coach will help you chart your own destiny and take a leap of faith based on your abilities. Believe in yourself. Recognize that if you are reading this book, you are one of the bold ones who tangibly represent the core spirit of American principles—personal responsibility for growth and development using yourself as the primary instrument of change. This is the ultimate in personal responsibility.

This book points you along certain paths. If you became lost while you were taking a motorcycle trip in a foreign country and had to stop to ask a farmer for directions, you could perhaps gain clarity through hand gestures and body language. Although this book will give you some excellent insights and general direction, it is your own positive motivation to complete the journey that makes the most difference. Self-improvement books are just the farmer.

Executives who improve even a little bit are more apt to continue their improvement. As soon as new skills are really integrated, a feeling of taking a step forward emerges. There is then motivation to continue. When a student learns a new math skill and then actually uses the skill to solve a problem, she is more motivated to acquire new skills. She sees the inherent power in that particular knowledge.

Even after you finish reading the book, you still will have blind spots. I know I do. But just knowing and acknowledging you have blind spots is a good thing.

There are many business coaches out there these days. The majority, however, do not possess doctoral degrees in psychology and counseling. Thus they are ill equipped to truly question the validity of statements made by the client. It takes years of professional education and experience to assimilate disconnected material and to interpret behavior on a deeper level. Thus, much discussion takes place in coaching, but little growth.

With most coaching relationships, there is a division of labor, so to speak. The client shares stories or relates a series of incidents, and the coach (supposedly) clarifies and helps interpret the events. Thus the client gains insight and grows. But when you "become your own business coach," you challenge yourself to make deliberate and accurate observations about *yourself*. You are put in charge of interpretations regarding yourself.

This isn't easy. But as the history of humanity clearly shows, people can and do grow. The task is infinitely more challenging today. Not too many generations ago, people didn't travel more than a hundred miles from their birthplace. Public information and education were minimal. Interpersonal encounters few. As a result, there was no compelling reason to understand oneself. Much more of life was lived, quite literally, in the dark.

Today's world is obviously the complete opposite. We are used to traveling all over the globe and being thrown together with different cultures, races, and values. We are inundated with information. The challenge of knowing yourself is more complicated, yet more important than ever.

Naturally, a highly trained coach will move you faster along in executive development than you can move yourself. Advanced degrees and years of experience count. But one shouldn't be in awe of specialists and professionals. You can grow without them. This book is predicated on this belief. Even mental health experts, when they try to analyze themselves, fall short like most laypersons. It is always the emotional blockages, not the intellectual blockages, that thwart us.

Two vital attributes of superior executives—an open mind and grounded self-esteem—stem from self-knowledge. Self-knowledge is strongly correlated with emotional stability. It is emotional stability that gives one steadiness under pressure, a capability to carry out successful conflict resolution, and the ability to handle criticism.

I believe self-knowledge is the unsurpassed and preeminent executive developmental strategy. It is through accurate self-knowledge that we develop the courage and emotional fortitude to go into the fire, right to the heart of a situation in an important dialogue. Going into the fire creates respect for a person as a leader. People know you have the emotional maturity to resolve human issues. If we don't reflect on our own behavior, we cannot exercise free will.

The book holds information—thought-provoking insights that help you work through the blockages that may keep you from manifesting your awesome potential. And what is the source of most of the information? Mostly you. You have much deeper knowledge and wisdom than you might give yourself credit for.

WHY DID YOU DECIDE TO READ
BECOMING YOUR OWN BUSINESS COACH?

What caused you to pick up this book? Perhaps it was your need to grow and develop. Developmental needs stem from unfulfilled desires. You may be experiencing a lack of realization or restriction that sparks change energy. Desires seek fulfillment. For example, when you're happy in your business life and you are firing on all cylinders, you generally don't seek improvement. But when you want real change, there is an aspect of your life, job, or career you find unacceptable. This restlessness prompts you to seek out change. You decide you want to be a member of the "high potential" team or you want to move to the next level, maybe even open up your own business. Perhaps there are long-term deficit areas you want to improve.

> *Fortunately analysis is not the only way to resolve inner conflicts. Life itself still remains a very effective therapist.*
> —Karen Horney

You can be thrust into a new, possibly uncomfortable situation as a result of job rotation, restructuring, mergers, or perhaps a performance appraisal. Maybe you have been let go from a job you enjoyed. Regardless of what causes you to be motivated, you are fundamentally tired of the status quo. You want to move on.

Let's take the position that you're feeling unfulfilled or dissatisfied with some aspect of your career. You want to become something more, unique, or different. You want to direct your own play and take command of your vocational life by improving your competencies. Take heart. Story after story describes people who, after being fired or let go due to "downsizing," go into a new situation and mature into a success far greater than the potential of what they left. Depending upon your attitude, progress after a so-called failure can be remarkable or minimal. In my life, I have found that my greatest successes occurred after my biggest disappointments.

For example, I was an executive in a series of venture-capital-backed deals, with every VC firm claiming they "partner" with management. After several ventures, I discovered that while a few venture capitalists had outstanding qualities, most brought surprisingly little to the table in terms of actually helping the company be successful. Rather, the senior management team partnership usually amounted to the VCs sitting around the boardroom table asking why sales weren't higher or overhead lower. I stopped waiting for a VC to fix the situation and put together a new business model fusing talent management with traditional venture capital competencies. This led me to greater success and career happiness. I stopped to assess the situation, examined it closely, and found a new and improved way of leveraging my talents.

Each of us has to make our way into the labyrinth of business life, and there are many paths to take, with concomitant land mines along the way. Self-knowledge helps us better navigate around these land mines.

If you want to make God laugh, tell him about your plans.
—Woody Allen

BE YOUR OWN TEACHER

Becoming your own business coach implies that you are your own teacher. View yourself as your student, your own higher self as your guide. Your higher self is what you could be if you overcame all the fears that hold you back and became the best you can be. If we remove doubts, we can know our essence. This is your "voice," the agent with whom you will communicate. It is not your "conscious" mind, the one who judges your actions and induces personal guilt. Instead, this is your ultimate best self, communicating with and advising your present self. When you are feeling positive, motivated, and optimistic, you believe in your capacity to achieve your goals. Tap into your higher self for advice and direction.

One advantage of personal self-improvement (as opposed to receiving professional coaching or attending retreats or classroom training) is that you are not attempting, consciously or unconsciously, to please your coach, boss, subordinates, or coworkers. Having led many executive training sessions, I have noted that many people are competitive, want to be better in the role plays, and so forth, in order to win favor or establish superiority. With self-development on your own time, at your own pace, through your own mechanisms, you are not seeking recognition or approval or affection. Thus the positive growth you make is for you and you alone. In its own way, this is honest and cleansing.

The observations and interpretations of a superior business coach are more accurate than our own observations. We are not impartial when we look at ourselves, often casting ourselves in a superior light. Standing opposite to this, though, is the fact we are more familiar with, and to, ourselves than any outsider could ever be. If you are motivated and desirous of personal growth, your examination of yourself can be outstanding and even objective.

The real challenge of executive growth is not an intellectual understanding of leadership, but rather the executive's resistance to accept the need for change. The crux of the matter is this: Through reading, writing, and self-analyzing your responses, are you able to overcome your own resistances? How much do you want to improve? The greater the desire for improvement, the greater the likelihood internal opposition will be overcome.

While other people can be valuable in helping us know ourselves, all too often they project their own inadequacies or fears onto us. They may send signals of limitations. I have heard parents say to their children, even when the "child" is fifty years old, "Don't expect too much" or "Anyone who aspires to greatness will be disappointed." The parent means well, but the advice is really a projection of his or her own fears. Don't discount valuable perspective, no matter where it comes from. But the key is validation. Does the criticism resonate with you? Has there been a pattern in your life to suggest the information is true?

One thing is for certain: Today's economic environment forces you to be quick and adept. There is increasing pressure to be proactive in managing your career. You are probably going to get downsized, get a knife in your back, get screwed over, and be out on the street at some point in your career. The ax isn't a negative anymore; welcome to the club.

Some people are satisfied with where they are in life. They may want to change, but their motivation is low; they are contented, all things considered. But I have found life more resembles a down escalator. If you are trying to just stand on a step and stay there, you still move downward, almost imperceptibly.

Other people just plain lack intellectual curiosity. The real work of introspection is a turn-off. They decide to "pass." Others are resistant to introspection because it smacks of feel-good psychology. These types usually have a repressed fear. Whatever the reason, there will be a percentage of people who are deliberately against taking any type of personality quiz or even talking about looking within. But you don't fall into this category; you're one of the courageous, driven ones. So . . .

GET READY TO WRITE

This book places you in control of your learning. An occasional burst of energy moves you through the chapters and exercises. What makes the book individual and personalized is that I ask you to write your thoughts at the end of each chapter—this activates and crystallizes your thinking while creating a valuable record of your progression of insights. The true reason to write is the increased possibility of recognizing yourself. This is active learning. The action is on your part; you are not just passively reading. When you write, you are engaged and thinking. You will be writing your ideas spontaneously and without censorship, thus creating a personal journal of sorts.

Consider *Becoming Your Own Business Coach* as a self-guided, personal introspective diary. The book is ultimately about making something good happen in your career. Unless you improve with actual results, the reading of the book is just an academic exercise—perhaps interesting, but not effective.

Right now, grab a pen. You're going to write down thoughts and reflections in response to open-ended questions. Don't cheat yourself by not doing this. Writing activates thinking. By the time you finish this book, you'll have written a brief, interesting, and personally meaningful journal. There is no right or wrong, only movement toward your success. Movement occurs when you believe it is possible for you to improve. Be your own biggest supporter and fan.

When you're finished with the book, reread your answers. See if you still feel the same. With the advantage of new thinking, analyze your original answers. Won't it be interesting to pick up the book a few years from now after progressing in your career and look back over your answers?

I'd advise you to get a notebook. Write your ideas and reflections on the thoughtful, challenging questions that are interspersed throughout each chapter, each marked by a ➔ symbol. Make it a personal journal. Someday, pick up the notebook and reread your own answers, in your own handwriting. This technique isn't new. But the twist is that *Becoming Your Own Business Coach* asks over a hundred open-ended questions that cause you to think seriously, carefully, and relatively calmly about your career and life. Thus, instead of a free-flowing, unstructured stream of conscious, you will write your life's plan—how to leverage strengths and succeed beyond your present career expectations.

2

Becoming More Introspective

As early as 1609, John Locke wrote, "Consciousness is the perception of what passes in a man's own mind, what is called reflective inner sense." Philosophers generally agree that looking within helps explain consciousness. William James, a famous founder of the field of psychology, remarked: "The word *introspection* need hardly be defined—it means, of course, the looking into our own minds and reporting what we there discover." American psychologist Edward B. Titchener emphasized training to improve the reliability and validity of introspection a century ago. We agree with his observation even today.

Introspection has been described as self-scrutiny; it is a process of direct personal observation or dialogue with the self. Introspection is personal; the privilege of the phenomenon is limited to one, and that one is you. You are uniquely positioned to articulate what you believe is true about you. You are always present to observe your own behavior. You are the preeminent authority. Nobody can ever know more about you than you.

> *"Introspection" is a term of art and one for which little use is found in the self-descriptions of untheoretical people.*
> —Gilbert Ryle

Treat your ability to examine who you are with honor. We humans are the only species capable of introspection. Introspection is not a choice we make, but a part of our genetic composition. All races and cultures are able to think about themselves. The choice is how to best harness this ability.

Executives, understandably, want to publicly minimize fears and weaknesses. They want to promote and receive recognition through their strengths. This is natural. There is competitiveness even in well-functioning corporate cultures. The advantage of this book is that you acknowledge weaknesses to yourself, with the inner realization that even if you could hide them from yourself, you really don't want to. That being said, it is uppermost to recognize that there is always a natural resistance to self-exploration. And we are generally not very quick to recognize our own personal resistances. The good news is that if we persist, and are even somewhat consistent in our effort to coach ourselves, our blind spots and resistances will eventually be recognized.

As a general principle, we tend not to introspect for causes of our psychological being when life is fundamentally going well. And why should we? Bills are being paid, the kids are doing well, our spouse isn't threatening divorce, the job is actually enjoyable, and the money good. But, as we all know, things change—often quickly and radically.

So be especially observant when things get out of kilter. If you feel stressed out, fatigued, irritated, fearful, or indecisive and you don't make any attempt at self-analysis, you are psychologically adrift. This is when executives can derail most quickly. Even though you are perfectly capable of doing so, you fail to look within for the meaning of your difficulty. You don't ask what you did to bring the negative energy into your life. Without introspection, you never arrive at a clear, aggressive pathway out of the problems.

Now for your first question:

→ When have you *not* introspected (at a time when, now looking from your present vantage point, you *should* have)?
→ How did the price you eventually had to pay increase because you didn't take time to sit down and really think?

All of us have life themes—"Been there, done that, got the T-shirt." Our themes are those issues that confound us fifteen to twenty years after they earlier derailed us or caused us significant trouble. For example, I have witnessed executives who have had some type of sexual harassment accusation leveled against them. Maybe they managed to work with Human Resources and got it dismissed. But the incident(s) caused personal turmoil and stress. And then the same thing happens again years later under similar circumstances.

At some point, this executive cannot help but question why hasn't he grown one iota in this regard in twenty years. He knows if he behaves in certain ways, there is an increased chance he will run into problems similar to those encountered twenty years earlier. Yet he does it anyway. The excitement or rewards of doing it outweigh the risks.

Ex-president Bill Clinton is an unfortunate example of this. Many people exclaimed at the time of his troubles that they expected more, how could he? and so on. Yet he had an issue with self-control. He had had similar problems earlier in his life that remained unresolved. The uproar helped derail his administration the last few years of his presidency. His unresolved issues took stature away and detracted from what is generally considered a successful presidency.

Life themes are frustrating. If you are over forty-five, you can readily attest to this!

→ What is your life theme? Have you noticed it coming back again and again in different ways, but similar forms?

There is some type of hidden factor that you resist looking at. But what? It is difficult to detect. The reinforcement or gratification you receive from your behavior is more powerful than your will to detect and overcome the root cause.

Some of the problem of your resistance may be the fact that whatever the root causes are, they are not very complimentary. Introspection invariably will come to negative conclusions about your character (or lack of it). So it's easy to see why there is a natural resistance to certain types of self-reflection.

It is most critical to understand resistances when you are passed over for a promotion, demoted, or fired (unless you were part of a wave of people let go because of economic downturn—although even here one could argue that if you had seen a way to uniquely add value, the company would not have laid you off). It is easier to be angry at the situation than to try to figure out what you could have done better or different. Generally, there is some time, maybe a year or two, of being angry before you are ready to objectively reflect. Moving out from the old environment, getting a new job, and becoming happy again all allow you to reflect with greater dispassion and clarity.

→ When have you received a career setback?
→ How long did it take to overcome your anger and look back with some level of detachment?
→ How did you improve as a result of new self-insight?

Even when we recognize shortcomings, we can acknowledge, with legitimacy, the rotten behavior people in our (past) environment inflicted upon us. In other words, in your introspection, it is all right to see snakelike qualities in coworkers who helped you fail. Those who have been in business for very long know that certain coworkers are scheming brown-nosers, that bosses can be mean-spirited asses, and that some company cultures amount to "every man for himself—screw teamwork." And in business life, you are going to occasionally get in the vortex of this malignant tornado. The point is not that you didn't legitimately get screwed. In fact, you probably did. But it is in your best interest to take any valuable lessons you can from your ordeal and move on. Being more successful than you ever could in your previous deal is the sweetest revenge of all.

→ When have you gotten screwed in your career?
→ Reflecting back on that event, what did you learn?

I had a client who was a partner in a consulting firm. High-level consulting firms are different than many other businesses. The people who are employed in consulting firms generally have substantial educational pedigrees and are highly analytical, at times egotistical. They are used to having decision-making freedom and acting independently. People are attracted to consulting firms because of the complexity of the assignments and the intellectual depth and rigor of the challenges that client companies pose. My client was offered a high-level executive position with one of his consulting firm's clients.

This scenario isn't unusual: You are consulting to a client and you are offered a position there. Happens every day. This was how I personally landed my first EVP job.

My coaching client was a genuinely good person. I thought the company who offered him the EVP position was fortunate to get such a bright, engaging, effervescent, and experienced person. He was considerate and empathetic and always tried to do the right thing. He was a team player, which is not necessarily the norm in a consulting firm.

Unfortunately, he joined a dysfunctional senior team. The executives were territorial, secretive, and guarded. You know there is a problem when senior executives begin sentences with "My guys think this" or "My team sees it this way." This strongly suggests factionalism and territorialism. (My client brought up this observation in one of our initial coaching sessions. I pointed out that this should have been his first clue the job was not going to be easy unless he could somehow figure out a way to lower the fences the executives erected around their functional areas.)

My client's job required cross-functional teamwork, a dynamic the senior team wouldn't—and indeed couldn't—provide. As you might already surmise, after about eighteen months, the board and the CEO decided it wasn't working out. My client was fired. He was bitter toward the executive team for not giving him a legitimate chance, and he was resentful toward the board and CEO for not helping him become successful.

His feelings are understandable. There is no doubt in my mind that the environment and his "team members" set him up to fail. I also thought the CEO was weak. He had not demanded better teamwork. He allowed the senior team to play stupid political games that reverberated down through the ranks, as it always does.

My coaching eventually got this executive to the point where he realized he didn't do enough due diligence about the opportunity. For example, he could have met with each team member before being hired to have in-depth discussions on how and why they would work together. That way he could have engineered their sense of involvement in the decision making. He could have talked with the CEO before he came on board about how the position, being new and cross-functional, would need the CEO's support.

My client had stars and dollar signs in his eyes. He didn't get all the facts and issues out on the table before he jumped at the opportunity. This sometimes happens in business life. We take a prospective offer that looks terrific on paper and are grateful and excited to get the chance of improving our lives and career. We then find, however, the situation was stacked against us.

In such cases, with introspection and looking back, we see that, although people acted without goodwill or fairness, we could have perhaps done more, too. The lesson? Remain as dispassionate as possible about heady career opportunities. Don't let your ego get the best of you. Take the time, if you can, to get buy-in from significant stakeholders. We resist these actions because we want to believe that the picture is as perfect as it (superficially) looks.

Still, in the spirit of tackling resistances, let's not be overly harsh on ourselves. When we see a goal, we form plans about how the goal can be achieved; we don't focus on the reasons why it can't be accomplished. Don't admonish yourself too much when looking back and seeing how psychological resistances to deeper introspection kept you from looking more objectively and deeper. You are not to blame for wanting to get ahead in life, for seeing an opportunity and going for it. Business environments are complex and hard to read. Even when we do our homework, we occasionally make mistakes. You can analyze something so much that you don't move fast enough. The point is that failures, roadblocks, and obstructions in our careers are often useful as growth mechanisms. But only if we allow them to be.

What are other resistances that are hard to personally detect that occur in your career? One is tedium, or being resigned or bored but refusing to grow or think of fresh ways to develop. You listlessly accept your job because you believe you cannot escape from your life situation. You feel hopeless because of your entanglements. You can't create enough incentives to move past your difficulties. You figure you are destined to be lower management or stuck in a position that is tolerable but not fulfilling. In essence, you have given up your expectations and the willingness to fight. In this situation, you can at least consciously be aware of your psychological state by saying to yourself, "Although I am bored and not fulfilled, I lack the motivation and willingness to sacrifice to change my status in life." This at least is being honest with yourself.

Another seemingly face-saving attitude is to take a philosophy-of-life approach and say, "Only guys who kiss ass get ahead," or "My boss doesn't like me, so I'm never going to get advanced," or "My personal situation doesn't allow me to maximize my abilities." While each statement may contain a grain of truth, they don't contain *all* the truth. By accepting a partial truth as the whole truth, you ruin the prospect of a more meaningful career.

I have observed people, as they get older and life gets no better, who become cynical or pessimistic about corporate life in general. When one is approaching sixty and finds oneself reporting to a thirty-eight-year-old, you can either get bitter or reflect on what you didn't do well that put you into that career path. Sometimes, it might be best to acknowledge that the younger executive is smarter, worked harder, is more ambitious, and deserves success. This doesn't negate you or your career, and it prevents or releases you from the psychological resistance of cynicism.

If a person has a general negative attitude, a cynical or depressed perspective of life in general, our coaching does little good. This psychological armor constricts psychological growth. One can go to leadership training and read numerous books on executive development, yet if a person is inwardly perpetually disparaging and skeptical, the exercise is purely academic.

A contemptuous executive can be sent to a leadership development class and be placed into a Myers-Briggs quadrant that describes him as ENFJ. However, this knowledge and descriptor will do nothing to change or develop the person. The psychological protectiveness is stronger than the new information. Emotions generally override and are stronger than a person's intellect. Cynical executives automatically say no to virtually every new idea or proposal. They think they are "realistic" and "bottom line." Hardly. They are projecting their own negative personality into business decision making. They unconsciously say no to new philosophies that shake up the existing psychological order.

→ When in life have you ever been cynical?
→ How did this affect your management or sales skills?

You only develop to the extent you don't have significant defense barriers. For example, if an executive has a neurotic need for power (and they are out there, as you well know!), professional coaching does virtually no good. The actual neurosis must be dealt with first. Dealing with true mental health issues is beyond leadership training. The vast majority of coaching efforts center on making good managers better.

Triumphing over others, winning at all costs, is the primary drive for the neurotically power-driven executive. Leadership training is looked upon with disdain. These executives are too organizationally savvy to verbalize this, of course. There is a whole collection of executives out there who still think personal development is "soft," designed for weak, timid, or ineffectual people. Feedback on how leadership could improve, how soft people skills could be better handled, is discounted.

The psychic forces that might have responded to the coaching are too enfeebled. These types are concerned with image. They demand to be seen as "successful." Feelings, thoughts, and behavior are driven by the outward establishment of superiority and impression. Friends are not friends; they are people to be used to promote agendas. This type of person does not truly sympathize with others even though he may give generously to certain charities. Giving is accompanied by much self-promotion and public displays of caring. Giving anonymously isn't part of the agenda. If the person has a conviction that he is a superior man, genetically endowed to win, why should he change?

POSITIVE INTROSPECTION

Introspection occurs on two levels. The first level is awareness of inner dialogue. We become attuned to the fact that we have the ability to communicate to ourselves. We do it anyway, but we just realize more directly we are doing it.

The second level is making judgments about the contents of our thoughts. When we say "judgment," we are not referring to condemnation or negatively labeling our thoughts. Rather, we refer to judgment in an improvement sense. For example, we might recognize and become aware from an inner dialogue that we are depressed about losing our job or important client. We say to ourselves, "I am depressed and anxious because I am afraid if I don't start making some money, I will lose my house and my kids won't be able to attend college."

Now, if we are able to tap into the richness and deepness of our higher self, we judge the introspective dialogue by saying: "I acknowledge my depression. But in this and every crisis lies opportunity. Let me think creatively to turn this negative into a surprisingly ambitious positive."

→ When have you ever turned a crisis into an opportunity, a negative into a positive?

Keep your thoughts on future goals. Continually visualize your ideal self and your focus here. When chaos hits, or when events go haywire (and they will), respond by saying, "I believe in the perfect outcome of every situation in life." Make your mind up to be joyful and unflappable. Resist the temptation to negatively respond. Disappointment is the pathway to becoming less fearful. In other words, when you experience disappointment and eventually overcome it you become stronger. Talk to yourself and others positively and optimistically. Understand that this is an ideal way of handling life. People who, for the most part, deal with life from this perspective are happier and more contented, in general, than others who worry and become depressed and bitter. Sometimes the only thing we can change is our attitude. But this emotional change creates a more positive energy that allows physical manifestation of change.

When adopting the habit of introspection, some people initially become more depressed or anxious. Some confusion and unhappiness may develop as you discover insights. But keep going! You will come through the growth to reach a higher level of self-satisfaction and comfort.

When we first begin anything, there is a period of uneasiness until we practice and progress. It is through our challenges, disappointments, and running into dead ends that we evolve and grow. Remaining optimistic when confronted by life's challenges is so important when you want to be a model for others to follow. As hard as it may be to believe, each roadblock is ultimately a unique and vital learning opportunity. Examine it, reflect upon it, and arrive at the realization that there is a hidden meaning in your frustration. This may sound naively optimistic, especially when down and out, but it is really the best way to handle life. One of life's greatest challenges is remaining optimistic. *Challenging ourselves through introspection and internal dialogue is an important antidote for depression.*

→ Think of an emotional situation you have experienced. Identify the emotion, and allow yourself to become aware of the feeling. Label it.

→ Now, judge your feeling. Challenge yourself to use this energy to become creative and resourceful about how else you could have attacked and gained victory over the issue. Describe the energy to yourself.

→ What is the thing you want to change most about your life?

→ What quality or qualities do you have that you *never* want to change about your life?

Self-knowledge, if it is acted upon, leads to self-renewal. In business, this is known as "continuous improvement." Let's take an example. Many people who consider themselves religious do not grow through religion. They engage in ritualistic worship without deepening or questioning. If you are to continue to grow, you must undergo constant development. This is true with faith, being a member of a profession, in sports, whatever. Everybody constantly has to work on improving their game or profession, or they just have "experience" but don't get better. As the often-repeated adage proclaims, "One can have twenty years of experience, or one year of experience twenty times." The difference is growth. Growth starts with self-examination.

AST believes that improved self-knowledge is a key ingredient for self-improvement. One cannot be substituted for the other. Introspection and the gaining of self-knowledge don't equate to self-improvement, but they set the machinery in place and the ball in motion.

Adults train children to express thoughts and feelings. As you progress in life, girlfriends or boyfriends, teachers, and peers teach you to express yourself with some degree of accuracy. There is ongoing training from your world in how to understand yourself. Age is valuable. You see yourself engage in behaviors, both good and bad, enough times to know the difference.

Over time, patterns emerge. Themes appear. These help identify a deeper sense of self. *Becoming Your Own Business Coach* is a catalyst for this activity. If you are following our recommendations, you have already started writing thoughts and answers in your journal.

Knowing yourself is quite possible. It is available to anyone and everyone. If we, as executives and entrepreneurs, remove our egos and defense mechanisms and are optimistic, we will improve. Executive growth is ensured. Be ruthlessly honest with yourself. Why not? What have you got to lose? That is the promise of this book. You have a better than "good" chance of self-realization and unlocking your special gifts and strengths by using the book as a guide.

Self-knowledge eliminates some of life's bad karma. You understand the real root of your actions. You are less self-delusional—bearing in mind that we are all partially self-delusional. When you know yourself well, you become wiser. Wisdom leads to better decisions.

Each of us is unique. *Therefore we have to ask ourselves unique questions.* Our challenge is figuring out what distinctive questions we need to ask. For example, you might ask:

- "How did my father's poverty when he was growing up later affect his altruism?"
- "How did my older sister's accomplishments cause me to doubt myself?"
- "What causes me to continually feel anxious even when things are going well?"
- "What causes me to resent authority?"
- "Why do I have a high need for recognition?"
- "Why do I have an excessive need for power?"
- "Why do I constantly have to rescue people?"
- "Why am I not more assertive?"
- "Why do I get stage fright so easily?"
- "What causes me to avoid forming long-term, loving relationships?"
- "Why can't I develop a life partner?"
- "Why do I use people and not have a single true friend, even though I am outwardly successful?"
- "Why do I make excuses for myself when I don't fulfill commitments that I have made to myself?"

You present your outermost thinking on a subject first. That is, if you are considering a topic, you say, "What is on your mind?"

Yet, as we all know, the more one talks about a topic, the more in-depth the thinking gets. The person taps into wisdom that she was not aware of. As she talks, the ideas that were swirling around in her mind become coherent enough to verbalize.

→ What are several distinctive questions you need to ask yourself?

We grow through life experiences by reflecting. Here are some occasions when I learn about myself:

• Reminiscing with an old friend
• Holding deep conversations with loved ones or close friends
• Driving a long, lonely highway all by myself with no radio on
• In the morning shower
• In an airplane staring out the window
• Infrequent but impactful dreams
• Evening walks around the block
• Looking at old photos
• Staring off into a beautiful view
• Sitting at a restaurant by myself having dinner on business trips

INTROSPECTION IS COGNITIVE

Introspection, at its core, needs to be seen for what it is: a cognitive/thinking knowledge source. Think about *introspect* as an action verb. It is something to be done, an action to be taken. Introspection is internal observation through internal dialogue. It is a cognitive achievement that takes effort. Thinking about yourself *to* yourself is a conscious mental and purposive process. You are aware you are thinking about yourself.

Here's an example. Let's say I become aware that I am tense. I pause to think about why. I decide that I feel trapped by deadlines and the possibility I will be singled out for public criticism. OK, that's why I feel tense.

Take another example. You're faced with a new job opportunity, so you *think* about it, the upside and downside. You imagine various scenes or possible situations and play these out in your mind's eye. This imagining is not introspection. *It only becomes introspection when you ask how you feel or what emotions you experience when you think about the new job.*

When executives think about something, they know how they feel about it. If they are asked whether somebody should be hired into a position, they form an opinion after proper interviewing, reference checks, and so forth. They go through some type of introspection and then arrive at a decision. *The clearer their introspection, the clearer their opinion.* This principle is always true. One of the important reasons senior executives are senior executives is the power of their introspection and the deepness of maturity the process creates.

Introspection means tearing away the outer layers of perception and examining more deeply your motives. It takes conceptual sophistication to know you are *aware* of your thinking. We think all the time, but introspection requires us to be aware of our thinking. Normally when we think, we don't think about thinking. Through introspection, we reflect on the content and accuracy of our thinking. Introspection produces beliefs that are dependent upon outer-sensory systems. In other words, what you see, smell, and hear combines to form an impression, which you then introspect on. Through this reflection, you form beliefs about your world.

Think of yourself as a scientific observer of your mind. Create an internal divide between the observer—you—and the object of study—your own thoughts. This is analogous to a professional counselor or a high-level executive coach. These professionals are paid to be the scientific observer of their client's mind. When introspecting, you perform the same function. The coach's advantage is that she listens and observes with objectivity. This is probably the biggest obstacle or hurdle to introspection. Your executive coach doesn't have bias. Awareness of partiality is an important first step toward objectivity and becoming your own business coach.

We take as self-evident that we have direct access to our mental state, but not to others' mental states. When you communicate within yourself, realize that *you* are talking to *you*. Only delusional people think thoughts can be sent to another person. You would be crazy to think another person could eavesdrop into your consciousness and listen to your thoughts, right? Indeed, the only entity many feel can listen to introspective communication is God. This concept and perspective is not far out or unusual. Indeed, if you remarked to a friend you were talking to God yesterday, he wouldn't dial 911. Most probably he would nod his head in agreement. Yes, he understands what it means to talk with God introspectively with the belief that God is listening.

This sets up a different view of introspection. It moves it into a spiritual dialogue. Let's not shy away from this subject or direction. God can hear our introspective discourse. If we try as best we can to be totally honest, open, and revealing in our dialogue with God, then good things come. Bad events continue, of course; that's the way of the world. But your reaction and ability to put them into context, to visualize a successful way out of your challenges, partially stems from the process of knowing yourself and being honest with yourself. Knowing yourself and your inner demons does not necessarily make you a better person. But it does make you a *wiser person*.

THERE ARE TWO OF YOU

Have you ever practiced a speech in front of a mirror? If you haven't, you really should, as it's a great way to overcome stage fright. When you do, you sense that there are two of you—the one looking into the mirror and the one looking back from the mirror. As you hear yourself speak, this separation becomes even more pronounced. Introspection is like this experience.

Take a moment now, look into a mirror, and talk out loud to yourself, just for fun. Notice how you feel like two people. Make deep eye contact. Ask the other you, "How are you doing today?"

See if you don't sense that there are really two parts: the outer person known to others, and the inner person known only to you. We accept that we are divided into two selves, one for the outside world, the second of our world.

You are simultaneously the object of study and the observer. Empirical scientists have issues with this, asserting that one cannot be unbiased when looking at oneself. But here, we dispense with this argument. We take the position that you *are* capable of being objective when looking within if guided by these exercises, knowledge, and your sincere motivation to want to become a better executive or entrepreneur. *Like all skills, over time and with practice, introspection improves.*

We know people make mistakes when they contemplate their motivations as to why they behaved the way they did. They usually aren't aware of their biases. In other words, people often really don't know why they behaved a certain way. They can describe their actions and how they felt, but they are less able to understand the deeper reasons why they did what they did.

→ Have you ever acted inappropriately and not known why? Looking back, can you self-diagnose? Was it a need for attention? Was it a way of getting back or getting even? Do you sense the way you acted was another person, not really you?

You believe what you believe about yourself even if your beliefs are challenged. If somebody describes us differently than we describe ourselves, we hold steadfast to our opinion. We don't argue with ourselves about ourselves. We rarely contradict ourselves. I hold the belief that I am a warm and engaging person. Why would I contradict this observation? I know it to be true. Some acquaintances might remark, "George is a cold, callous person." Perhaps my relationship with *them* is aloof. We don't connect. Each prefers emotional distance. From their perspective, I am cold. But this conclusion is fundamentally wrong. And I know it. We understand that the majority of people experience a certain part, usually a selected part, of ourselves. We present our social self as we want others to perceive us. We have an internal evaluation and description of ourselves.

→ In what way would you portray yourself to yourself?
→ How would your worst enemy describe you?
→ Is there any truth to this enemy's description? Or is he or she looking through biased eyes?

LIMITATIONS OF INTROSPECTION

The problem of personal insight is one of the deepest and most difficult ones in philosophy and psychology. Experimental psychologists often dismiss introspection. Seeing directly into people's minds isn't possible. Introspection, by its very nature, cannot be verified by the usual and customary scientific methods, so scientists shrug their shoulders and say the concept doesn't hold enough scientific validity. Of course, it is meaningful to the person who engages in it.

I appreciate the adage, commonly expressed in my profession, "If it exists, it can be measured." With increased sophistication of brain wave studies, introspection will someday be measurable. But we exist in the here and now. We need to improve now. So, let's not wait for outside validation. We already know that the more we reflect on our lives, question our thinking, challenge ourselves to deliberate differently, and analyze where we've made errors in our logic, the stronger leaders we become.

As we discussed earlier, it's challenging to acknowledge that not all of what we think about ourselves is correct, but we, through self-knowledge, can reduce life's misattributions. In order to obtain self-knowledge, one must introspect at least to some degree. Let's take a typical example.

Suppose you have a career that is going pretty well. Not great, but OK. You decide to stick it out with your employer. You hope over the long haul that your talents and contributions will be recognized. After ten years, you have progressed, but you aren't on the fast track. Your job looks as secure as it can in today's world. Yet others have been promoted over you. You're not really going anywhere.

Upon deeper reflection, you recognize it was the fear of moving to a new job at a new company, starting new relationships, new thinking, new everything, that caused you to hold back from exploring opportunities. In reality, upon introspection and self-reflection, it was not your contentment with your job or your "loyalty" that compelled you to stay. It was fear of change. In actuality, you were scared of interviewing and being rejected. Unfortunately, you were not conscious of this until ten years had blown by.

We can look back at our lives and see, after ten years of time, that more than we care to admit was ego-based illusion. We believed what we wanted to believe. So while we *thought* we had engaged in introspection, our conclusions were woefully inaccurate. This doesn't mean we should stop introspecting; we have to because we are human. However, we need to be mindful that many of our conclusions are false. We don't take our biases, prejudices, and self-esteem into account.

> *Ten years have come and gone, no one told you when to run . . .*
> *you missed the starting gun.*
>
> —Pink Floyd

➔ Reflect upon a time in your life you believed something to be true. Now, after ten years, you know you were self-delusional. How did *wanting* something to be true distort the truth?

➔ How did your misdiagnosis affect your life?

Our point? None of us is infallible when self-reflecting. What you thought was true, over time, proved to be self-inflicted illusion. The bad news? When you are trying to figure out how you really feel about a situation, there are delusions, forgetfulness, wishful thinking, deceit, and fantasy. The good news? Through your contemporary introspection, you now know, really know, what is holding you back. Now you're in a great position to burst free. Ideally, it is this high level of objectivity we want to exhibit within ourselves to ourselves all the time. But note the key word "ideally." It's not going to happen as much as we want!

Introspection needs validation, but how does one go about validating? Bottom line: *Through events unfolding as you predicted or agreement from unbiased observers.* In other words, things you introspected about work out according to plan. That lets you know you are doing something right; you analyzed your situation correctly and took appropriate actions.

Have you ever been wrong? Of course. Anybody who says no is obviously delusional. Before you realized your misstep(s), you were under the false assumption your thinking and planning were right. That doesn't mean you suddenly don't trust yourself—although at times we can lose self-confidence. But you begin to acknowledge when you consider something that your consideration could be wrong.

You are limited in what you evaluate. Some variables you understand and take into account. And there are other variables that may have revealed or partially revealed themselves, but you were, and are, not self-perceptive enough to pick up on them.

We will make mistakes even when it appears the balls on life's pool table are lined up to run the table. It's the proverbial unexpected event that screws us up. But sometimes that event, in hindsight, was preventable. We just made a series of mistakes in analyzing the situation. Our own constitutional weakness was the real culprit that caused the situation to go askew.

Another criticism of introspection is that human beings often misidentify the reasons they feel a certain way. For example, Angela may say Bill really upset her, when it was really a series of events earlier in the day that had Angela stoked to explode in anger. She doesn't mentally connect the dots. The dots are in her unconscious, and she can't connect them. Thus, Bill gets yelled at for a pretty small infraction. He is confused about where Angela is coming from.

> ➔ What is a time where you got angry at a situation, but it was actually other factors that really caused your outburst?

As a general rule, we do not ask ourselves how we feel unless we are in a state of depression or anxiety sufficient to cause us to acknowledge to ourselves, yes, we are miserable. One of the benefits of going through tough times is it causes us to straighten out our priorities. We do our growing while recovering from events.

> ➔ When have you gone through some tough times?
> ➔ What did you learn about yourself?

INTROSPECTION RESULTS IN
BEHAVIORAL CHANGE

We try to understand ourselves through analyzing past behavior. Private data, data in our own minds, cannot be validated *except* by behavior. Indeed, it is only by analyzing our past actions and behavior that we see the patterns we interpret.

→ What lessons have you had to relearn and relearn again?

We create our own version of who we are, which contains much truth. However, our version also contains what we *want* to believe about who we are. When we look within, we can kid ourselves. We may not be aware of all the dynamics that cause us to be untruthful. We are not consciously "lying." We may in fact be convinced our self-reflections are accurate. It's just that they are often not. *Ultimately we have to analyze our behavior, not our intentions.*

When you are aware of your responses to stimuli, try to understand your own behavior, and consciously acknowledge how you feel to yourself, you gain better access to your own underlying reasons for behavior. Experience is the accumulation of cause and effect. Over time, there is an internal validation when you reflect on your behavior.

Introspection in and of itself is not the goal. Producing positive actions and behaviors is. Most psychologists agree that, if you change behavior, then over time attitudes and habits change.

We try to understand people through their behavior. We can't read their minds, only observe their conduct. This concept is what ushered in behavioral interviewing in the 1970s in organizational and industrial psychology. Dr. Paul Green, the renowned psychologist who coined the term "behavioral interviewing," emphasizes past performance and behavior to predict future behavior. Behavioral interviewing stresses that the past predicts the future. If two situations are fundamentally similar, the best way to predict a person's behavior, performance, outcome, and results is by looking at what the person did the first time around. Most of AST's clients use the theory and practice of behavioral interviewing to one degree or another.

Preparing yourself for a challenging job interview leads to introspection. For example, below are several behavioral interviewing questions we often ask job candidates at AST. Through this exercise, we are not trying to prepare you for a job interview. Our point is that when you prepare for a behavioral interview, you invariably go through introspection. Read these questions. Mentally answer them. Note as you read each question that you generally need 7 to 10 seconds before you respond with clarity. This brief reflection is a form of introspection. You have to think through your answers.

- Give me an example of a time when your positive attitude and sales skills caused others to be motivated to use you instead of the company they had been using.
- Give an example of a time when you were able to build rapport with a client when you had to make a tough sales pitch even when the situation was a difficult one and the odds were against you.
- Tell me about a specific experience of yours that illustrates your ability to influence a possible client. Feel free to use an example that involves changing an attitude, selling an idea or program, or being persuasive.
- Being empathetic to clients' problems requires you to take extra care to understand their circumstances or predicament. Give me an example of a time when you were able to understand a client's unique issues because you put yourself in his shoes. How did your ability to recognize his emotional issues contribute to a successful outcome?
- If you are going to be successful in a human capital–type industry, you have to display great skill and care with clients. Share several examples of when you built a long-term relationship with a client and she turned to you for advice and counsel that pushed your relationship into the friendship category.
- Tell me about a time when your reflective listening skills allowed you to peel the layers of the client's issues until the core problem was revealed. What was the real issue, and how did you address it?
- Tell me about a time when you were willing to disagree with a client in order to build a positive outcome.
- Describe a time when you had to discuss the "elephant in the room" with a critical client. What did you say? How did you get up the courage to be direct and talk with candor?
- Tell me about a time when you were in a competitive environment and were successful.
- Creative thinking means putting aside the tried and true in order to allow new, fresh energy to be focused on the challenge. When have you been able to break out of a traditional way of looking at a problem and shine a fresh light on it?

- Creativity often means stepping back from a regimented way of thinking. When have you been able to break out of a structured mindset and intuitively play with new concepts and ideas?

HOW YOU MISINTERPRET

When you observe others' behavior, you can contaminate your interpretation of their behavior through your own defense mechanisms and filters. Knowing the other person can help or hurt our accuracy in decoding his or her actions. For example, if ten people observe a person doing something, there will be various and conflicting accounts of what, how, and why he did it. Additionally, when playing armchair psychologist, much of our interpretation is projected by our own personality—a fact most are oblivious to. We project our own needs, wishes, paradigms, and ego into our observations. If you don't know the other person and are merely asked to observe behavior, you are often objective. This is what good professional interviewers do—objectively observe behavior and evaluate a job candidate's answers to questions.

> *But behavior in the human being is sometimes a defense, a way of concealing motives and thoughts, as language can be a way of hiding your thoughts and preventing communication.*
> —Abraham Maslow

The less mentally healthy you are, the less accurate your introspective judgments. If you suffer from mental health issues, your introspection is likely to be erroneous. For example, when a paranoid introspects, he is going to arouse suspicion even though there is no verifiable evidence that anybody is out to get him.

Your introspective judgments are subject to as much error as your degree of accuracy in the perception of your world. If you are constantly misperceiving the reality of your world, then introspective analysis of your thoughts is going to have a corresponding amount of error variance. When a person has an absence of accurate self-knowledge, her likes and dislikes determine her beliefs.

All of us engage in some level of self-deception, sometimes in the face of clear contrarian evidence. You never *intend* to trick yourself, but we do it all the time. Freud said the unconscious may mislead the conscious self to keep painful events, facts, and ideas repressed. We revise or overlook facts that are contrary to what we want to believe. This is a sobering thought.

> *It's not what you don't know that gets you into trouble; it's what you know that just ain't so that gets you into trouble.*
> —Satchel Paige

Your insights stem from the limited amount of information you can hold in your short-term memory and recollections you retrieve from long-term memory. The key is to cognitively address your conscious. Over time, you "remember" other memory fragments important to insights. How well you objectively ask yourself questions and are truthful determines how much good information you get. The better you encode information, the better your output will be. Remember the old saying with computers "garbage in, garbage out"? It is the same concept with introspection.

Introspection is reliable when you ask yourself earnestly and honestly what is causing or shaping your behavior. There will always be repression of unwanted material causing distortion. But honest, healthy introspection does lead to truth at a level that is more than acceptable.

3

Becoming Aware of Your Path

UNDERSTANDING YOUR STRENGTHS

Most Americans do not know what their strengths are. When you ask them, they look at you with a blank stare, or they respond in terms of subject knowledge, which is the wrong answer.

—Peter Drucker

The more you know about yourself, the more you understand true passions. The easiest and best way to enjoy career success is to know, understand, and leverage strengths. For example, if you have the ability to concentrate for long hours on minutiae and connect the dots, your focus should be research and long-term project work. Collecting and refining data is a laborious process. When done correctly, insights into consumer behavior or products are mined. Companies pay well for these statistical gems.

Let's say you're creative and truly think outside the box. Going into some type of design or strategic marketing role is right for you. An advantage of a unique, one-of-a-kind creative personality is that companies will pay a luxury price tag.

If you have a flair for social functions and make things flow seamlessly, then becoming an event planner is a good route.

I think every person should be able to enjoy life. Try to decide what you most enjoy doing, and then look around to see if there is a job for which you could prepare yourself that would enable you to continue having this sort of joy.

—Linus Pauling

Perhaps as an adolescent, you had a natural liking for working on cars. You liked it and you were good at it; you were good at it, so you liked it. You took auto mechanic courses in high school as an elective. You loved them. You decided to major in engineering in college and focus on producing new green cars. You understood what you are naturally good at and wedded it to formal education in a growing field. This is the best way to ensure your career, long term.

Some people know they're good with engines. Even as kids, they could fix bicycles. Intuitively they knew which way to turn wrenches. They grow up tinkering, spending hours disassembling an engine to see what's wrong with it and understanding how it works. When these people go in the career of modifying cars for racing enthusiasts, they know they bring something special. They know what they're talking about.

All of us have abilities we've always known we possess. The form of the ability might have evolved, but the core strength is there from the beginning. By going into the career route or by shaping your job so your core dimensions are maximized, you'll be more assured of a lifelong fascination with your job.

There's always a concealed, unseen cause that precedes any event. Seeds are planted. But when there's a significant gap of time between what you plant and what you eventually sow—whether good or bad—the connection may not be readily apparent. This is true for many situations. The event seems random until you carefully trace its origins. Then you begin to see subtle connections.

For example, a person doesn't suddenly decide to become a top salesperson out of the blue. Many leaders start in sales because selling is an excellent way to measure results, and research shows top performers like being measured. Perhaps as a child you were a hustler. Did you have a doughnut route where you went door to door trying to sell a box of doughnuts? How about a lawn-cutting or babysitting service that was more than an occasional odd job? Maybe you had a nice little business going.

Knocking on doors or making "sales calls" when young is a great way to emotionally toughen up. Tough-mindedness and emotional resiliency are important—even more so when you have a territory or area you continuously call on. You understand resistance and rejection. You're not just collecting for the Girl Scouts or the Heart Association on a one-time basis. You go back over and over again to the same people. Slowly, even though you've been rejected twenty times, on the twenty-first knock, you get a sale. Fortitude and perseverance eventually paid off. These events leave a deep positive, psychic residue.

Early business experiences and successes set future sales-driven leaders apart from people who don't hang tough over the first year with few sales and little feedback and commissions.

They push the panic button, get scared, and jump to a safer, more predictable, and less risky environment.

Let's take another example. How about the child who loved art, showing aptitude for it in kindergarten? Her horses were always the best. Her portraits resembled the people she was drawing. When she decided to go into a graphic design career, she knew that what she was providing was creative and distinctive. She doesn't doubt her ability to offer her internal or external clients something original and interesting. She has confidence to showcase her talent.

How about the person who is sensitive, cares deeply about his fellow human beings, and has a reverence for God? He knows he wants to go into the clergy and spread the good word. Some of the best leaders I've met are church ministers, rabbis, and pastors who've built large, committed congregations. The power of their belief in the vision of what their church or synagogue could become, and their ability to sell that vision, is an unstoppable force.

The simple lesson? It's obvious. Try and try to pursue a career in which, over your life span, you've known you were genetically hardwired for. Concentrate on talents and abilities. Dwell on strengths, not weaknesses. Realize there are certain things you are really talented at and do exceptionally well. When you're good, you have a repertoire of strategies for accomplishing goals.

> *Choose a job you love, and you will never have to work a day in your life.*
>
> —Confucius

Recognize core strength. This is harder than it appears. AST has many clients, well into their forties, who privately share that they really don't understand their true strengths. This is where positive psychology plays such an important role. Positive psychology gets people to think back on their lives and ponder what came easily and naturally to them.

→ Thinking back on your childhood, what came easily and naturally to you? (This is most probably your greatest strength.)

This knowledge in and of itself has value. You feel powerful when you utilize natural strengths. No longer are you at the mercy of forces that are more powerful than you.

→ Concrete knowledge of your strengths provides a realization that there is a chance to *do* something with those strengths. What factors contributed to your abilities?

HOW DO YOUR STRENGTHS FIT IN WITH OTHER ASPECTS OF YOUR PERSONALITY?

You exist within genetic and cultural parameters. By the time you're seven, core personality traits are embedded. Accept you for who and what you are. But have an open mind and a willingness to expand natural capabilities. Biology isn't destiny. Always challenge yourself to grow. When we expend effort toward those things we are naturally good at, our growth trajectory is steeper.

For parents, genetic programming resonates. If you've raised several children from birth and observed them evolve throughout their lives, you know "they were born that way." As your life unfolds, your core traits remain constant and even solidify. Hopefully these traits temper and mature with age and experience. However, there is increasing evidence that emotional and behavioral competencies can be developed over time, which is a purpose of this reading experience.

CLAIMING YOUR STRENGTHS THROUGH YOUR WEAKNESSES

→ To claim your unique strengths, list your weaknesses. Complete these phrases that point toward things that give you difficulty:
- I can't . . .
- I can only . . .
- I can never . . .

Notice the negative characteristic of these formulations?

→ Now imagine each negative statement you wrote represents a talent camouflaged as a weak point. What is the hidden skill in each? Ask yourself what's different about you compared with those who don't possess each of these characteristics. Then write a counterpart expressing the concealed strength. Examples:
- I can't learn software programs very quickly—but what I lack in concentrated logical thinking, I more than make up for in my emotional intelligence.
- I can only do one thing at a time—but when I do something, it's done with thoroughness and competence.
- I can never come up with a quick comeback when I'm challenged—but I like to think issues through and not be

glib and shoot from the hip. This gives me credibility over the long run.

Psychological strength means accurately acknowledging limitations and biases. Knowing, understanding, and accommodating weaknesses gives personal power. Weaknesses are challenges, "opposite strengths" compensated for by true strengths. *You're most emotional and self-protective where you're weakest.*

To view yourself clearly requires reflection and examination of judgment. The idea is to retain self-confidence but with courage to criticize your standpoint. Admit your point of view's relativity. You then recognize your weaknesses and take them into account in decision making. When you do, you generate superior analysis and improve decision-making quality.

→ How are your strengths the opposite of your weaknesses? How are your weaknesses the mirror image of your strengths?
→ In what areas would you most like to improve?
→ What must you do differently to develop weaknesses into strengths?
→ How have weaknesses affected your career?
→ What do you really want most from your career?

The only true way to measure achievements and progress is to make a decision to set goals, both business and personal.

→ How do you define success?
→ What are the realistic options in your life? (Don't let this question squelch your personal vision, however!)

Work backwards in time.

→ What do you want your life to look like in twenty-five years?
→ In fifteen years?
→ In ten years?
→ In five years?
→ In one year?
→ In six months?

SIGNIFICANT EXPERIENCES AND MOMENTS

There are events and significant life moments that have molded your perception and definition of what it means to be a leader.

Although these events might seem minor to an outside observer, these incidents, for whatever reason, stick in your memory. They form the nucleus of your attitudes toward leading and managing.

I remember one incident in my teenage years. I was sitting in the kitchen eating—I was always eating as an adolescent—and my father's boss called. My father got lambasted for some infraction. I watched as my father cringed and repeatedly said "Yes, sir" to the boss. Although I didn't understand the effect this vignette would play on me, I knew at that point I wasn't crazy about the idea of having a boss. My streak of entrepreneurialism was no doubt fertilized by this significant experience. My disdain for bosses who use intimidation and dominance as their management style germinated in that moment. Yelling at employees says a lot more about the lack of self-control than it does about the ability to motivate.

Here's another personal example from my teenage years. I was caddying golf clubs to make a few bucks, back when golf carts weren't the norm. At the end of a round, I loaded the clubs into the trunk of a shiny new Cadillac. The gentlemen for whom I had been caddying handed me a crisp ten dollar bill and told me I had done an excellent job. I thanked him for his generosity. The usual pay for toting clubs around for eighteen holes was a whopping five dollars, so this was double the going rate. He replied, "Son, work for yourself, it's a lot better!" That statement got lodged into my brain. It remains there many years later.

Isn't it interesting when I contemplate why I like entrepreneurs and small business owners so much that it comes back down to these two events, even though they appear innocuous?

→ Reflecting back, what memories and experiences have inspired you?
→ Have you watched a particularly effective executive? What did she do well that you would like to emulate?
→ Conversely, have you experienced a particularly terrible executive? What did he do that you would like to avoid emulating?

LOOKING AT YOUR PERSONAL CULTURE

All of us come from some type of culture, the place of our environment. When people grow up in a certain culture, they tend to have common experiences. Let's examine yours, as defined by Geert Hofstede's five dimensions of cultural personality. As you read these five dimensions, reflect on how you were brought up. What was your family's socioeconomic status, and how has this affected you?

Think about the entire society and country you grew up in. Consider the values that were passed to you. For example, I grew up in an intact family in a mostly white, middle-class area. The values I grew up with included hard work; my mother's favorite expression was "The Lord helps those who help themselves." Honesty was stressed. Progressive, nonjudgmental values were, too. I picked up emotional-intelligence mentoring from my father, who had a remarkable amount of interpersonal skill. He was a professional engineer, no less. Not surprisingly, all of my daughters hold similar beliefs. As one daughter insightfully said, "You believe what your parents believe." Wise and thoughtful, considering she was eight.

Hofstede's dimensions are described below.

Power Distance

How much did your home culture accept and expect that power is distributed unequally? In the United States, we accept that control is hierarchical. Money means power. We created big corporations with bureaucracy. Rank means power. If you have worked for a big company, you understand how power is distributed from the CEO on down. The corner office or "C Suite" symbolizes power distance.

Entrepreneurs often don't like authority and power controlling them. This drives them to go into business for themselves. The one concept that unifies America is: we all want our own business. We are truly a nation of entrepreneurs. I personally believe this is perhaps our greatest cultural strength.

In the United States, it is my observation that we are evolving into more innovative business cultures. Power is less important than innovation through employee engagement. Within the information technology sector in the late 1980s, there was a deconstruction of rank. Companies valued creativity and the power of thought. Everybody agrees that good ideas can come from anywhere and everywhere in companies, yet it took electronic communications to change the hierarchical management style of the industrial revolution. Through the power of IT, we stripped out middle managers whose main job was collecting information to pass to upper management. Communication, data collection, and analysis are now vastly more efficient.

There are still plenty of authoritarians lurking out there. About 25 percent of the general population has authoritarianism embedded into their personality structure. But the old-line industries that use this style are dying. The evidence is obvious when a company or country has high power distance. Where there are clear lines between the haves and have-nots, dissatisfaction grows. Union distrust, the executive dining room with all the perks, unusually large pay differentials, parking spaces, different floors in buildings, and the like all create a type of culture and thinking. Some power differential is necessary, but it is when the power turns dysfunctional and repressive that conflict starts. With the financial meltdown of 2008–2009, Wall Street excesses came into scrutiny and disfavor. Greed and indulgence became increasingly out of style.

→ How much do you tend to speak up around authority?
→ Do you think the company you work for, or used to work for, has a large power distance?

Individualism vs. Collectivism

The United States has the Horace Greeley "Go west, young man"–type thinking embedded in our collective psyches. We espouse individual responsibility for our actions and achievements, or lack thereof. We know our neighbors. They are responsible for themselves. We are responsible for ourselves. The *individual* is the driving force in our society. Collectivist societies and cultures, on the other hand, integrate people into strong "in-groups." For example, these can be extended families that help children into the game and allow them to grow within the system. The price tag? Unquestioned loyalty. Take our forty-third president, George W. Bush, as an example of an in-group member. One of his failings as a CEO was that he prized loyalty over competence. This stemmed from his upbringing of being part of a rich political dynasty, a "collectivist" family.

→ How much of your beliefs about getting ahead come from taking personal responsibility?
→ Who gave you advice or helped you get a break?

Masculinity vs. Femininity

In some societies, both sexes are modest, peaceful, and nurturing. Men are more feminine and are OK with it. In other societies and cultures—notably, U.S. business culture—assertiveness and competitiveness, even to the point of aggressiveness, are valued. Dominance is still a personality trait predictor for success in

American business. In the United States, we value competitive people. This might be changing, however, as the value of teams is proven more powerful than star individual performers, especially where a lot of valuable partnering is important. Address the following two questions and see if you are more masculine or more feminine in your approach. There is no right or wrong; at times you need both.

→ Do you like and value coaching, nurturing, and helping people or do you prefer being individually bold and decisive with people?
→ Do you like leaders with an inclusive communications orientation or those who set clear direction?

Uncertainty Avoidance vs. Tolerance for Uncertainty

In some countries and businesses, uncertainty and ambiguity are accepted and even relished. In others, they are avoided: Employees follow the manual. There is only one truth. There is rigidity and adherence. As in family dynamics, people that stem from uncertainty avoidance are more emotional and anxious. When there is tolerance for ambiguity, openness, and relativism, you are at peace with variability. When a company is run by processes (and there is nothing wrong with this—many great companies are, in fact, a series of processes), there is a low tolerance for uncertainty. A good manufacturing company or a fast food company should be run primarily by processes. When you are running a more creative business, you need a high tolerance for uncertainty; you want people thinking, exploring, testing, and forming lots of hypotheses.

→ Do you tend to like ambiguity or more certainty?
→ Under what conditions do you thrive?

Long-Term vs. Short-Term Orientation

Long-term orientations are more reflective of Eastern societies. Age, the length of time a society has been in existence, honoring the past generations genealogically, and valuing perseverance and thrift are held in esteem. Short-term societies value institution, custom, and social obligation. We all agree that quarterly earnings and the smoothing of accounting to meet expectations are not healthy ways to look at companies and sectors. Yet we keep doing it because our U.S. culture centers on the short term.

→ Do you see the long-term vision of your career? Are you overly focused on the short term?

→ On my "career gravestone," I would like it to read . . .

USING PERSONALITY TESTING

Many companies offer management training where people go to classes and take short profiles such as Myers-Briggs or Firo-B and have them interpreted by a certified trainer. These are sometimes useful, sometimes not. If you go with an open mind and just try to learn something about yourself, the classes, for the most part, do some good. One of the positives about personality testing is you can compare your scores to those of other people. This provides a frame of reference.

Personality tests are useful to understand yourself. Some of the older standardized tests were initially developed almost a hundred years ago. They have been slowly and carefully developed into better and better instruments. There are all sorts of personality tests available, with widely varying levels of well-researched norms holding predictive validity.

The idea of trying to understand people by describing their personality dates back to Hippocrates (c. 450 BC). He classified people into one of four categories, depending on the kind of fluid that they had in their bodies. This began the idea of describing temperaments. Wilhelm Wundt in the late 1800s described the distinction between the human body and personality. Interestingly, the broad descriptors even today generally come down to four or five types, as they did to Hippocrates.

Over the past generation, with larger meta-analytic studies, personality theorists have described what is now called the "Big Five" theory of personality. Basically, personality researchers say there are five basic broad areas or dimensions of personality:

1. *Extraversion.* This trait denotes people who are more naturally social. They enjoy interaction and the giving and receiving of emotional bonding. They strike up conversations in lines, on airplanes, or wherever and approach people easily at social gatherings. People with extraversion naturally move toward people. Contact with others actually energizes them. Salespeople and some professional services consultants often have a lot of extraversion.
2. *Agreeableness.* This personality dimension is about getting along and subordinating your ego to mold to the group's

dynamics. You usually don't assert your opinion, interrupt others, or point out disagreements within the discussion. It includes attributes such as kindness, trust, affection, altruism, and other pro-social behaviors. People who have a kindly disposition and can resolve conflict and get along well in teams have this dimension. As globalization demands more virtual global teaming, this trait is becoming a valuable one. Among the Big Five, agreeableness correlates least with effective leadership in many studies, however. Sometimes overly agreeable people don't want to ruffle feathers, so they take the path of least resistance in conflict management. This dimension is useful for customer service people.

3. *Conscientiousness.* This trait denotes people who stick to the plan and processes. They control their emotions. They stay on task. Organization and the ability to lay out the steps useful to reach a goal are common features. They also show high levels of thoughtfulness, goal-directed behaviors, and control of impulses. They tend to be organized and mindful of details. They get things done, make things happen, follow through, set deadlines, and complete the mission on time and under budget. People who like order and like set criteria are often conscientious. For instance, accountants usually have this ability; they honestly like closure, measurement, and exactness.

4. *Emotional stability.* Individuals showing this trait tend to experience emotional constancy, steadiness, and grace under pressure and can deal with stress effectively. Emergency room physicians and people who must make a lot of quick decisions with conflicting information do better when they have an inner calmness and balance. For example, a person who scored low on emotional stability would be more used to getting into altercations because of a low ability to tolerate frustration. The degree of your ability to prevent erratic behavior is dictated by you. You decide to allow yourself to become easily frustrated. Counseling, self-monitoring, and training can help you to become better adapted. Emotional stability is important for leadership—you don't want an emotionally reactive person in charge.

5. *Openness.* Openness is the receptivity to new experiences and searching for other ways to consider or think about the issue. Open people have varied interests. They can analyze opposing thoughts about the same subject and come up with a unique third approach. They are imaginative and insightful and tend to have a broad range of interests. Artistic and

creative types have a lot of this dimension. People who like to think outside the proverbial box and who come up with interesting approaches and twists are often open-minded and nonjudgmental.

→ Now, here's a fun and useful exercise. Rank-order your personality dimensions. All dimensions are good, but force yourself to rank them. What is your "top" dimension? Now work your way down.

Whatever your top two dimensions are in the above exercise, try to mold your career around them. For example, if you are high in extraversion and openness, going into a human interaction business such as consulting with a strong dose of innovative problem solving could be rewarding. If you have taken a number of personality tests and you generally scored high on introversion and conscientiousness—which means you favor more detail-oriented processes with a high sense of order—you might reflect and move your career into project management or process reengineering. If you ranked yourself high on emotional stability, you could work in a job that has a high stress level; you have the ability to let stress roll off your back better than most. If you are high in openness, you tend to appreciate creativity and originality, so an innovative environment and job would be best for you.

→ How does your job tap into your highest-ranked personality dimension?
→ How could you alter or develop your current job to tap into your highest dimension?
→ How can you fashion, or mold, your work environment so it plays more naturally to your top two dimensions?

Personality traits generally remain stable throughout a person's lifetime. In other words, by the age of seven there are broadly defined character traits that come to be embedded in our personality.

For example, let's say as a child you had a tendency to be outgoing and comfortable with being on stage. This may include extraversion (although there are plenty of introverted entertainers), a healthy self-esteem, and an animated, open, gregarious style. At forty, your associates would probably describe you in much the same way. Even though you aged, your core personality should hold. If somebody has patience and concentration, it's unlikely they will lose these traits as they age. The idea of changing your core personality is a daunting one. Early on, we get hard-wired.

The important thing is to understand what your core traits are. Figure out how to best use them to further your career. I believe our core personality traits are more genetic than learned, although there are plenty of psychologists and behavioral scientists who disagree. Let's not debate the issue. The fact is, by the time you read these words, you are what you are. The game now is to understand your strengths and develop a career path and find a company that values you.

Tests may have a large number of statements or adjectives where the respondents rate the applicability of each item to themselves. Over a sizable number of questions, a person tends to fall into descriptors. For examples, traits measured are "extroverted" compared to "introverted," "social" or "distant," "emotionally stable" or more "volatile," "open to change" or "conservative," "organized" or "disorganized," "agreeable" or "disagreeable," "sensitive" or "tough minded."

Sometimes ipsative responses—norms you use to measure yourself—ask you to choose between two equally good responses that place you into some type of box. For example, "I like to work closely with people" versus "I enjoy a good intellectual debate." This is useful to find a career fit, discovering your personality high points to better understand what work situation might be best for you, or improving relationships by better understanding coworkers. All kinds of tests are available online to measure if you are an optimist or pessimist, your level of egoism or altruism, your locus of control (how much you believe you control what happens to you in life), how sensual you are, and more. Feel free to take any number of these online tests and read your results.

The goal is not self-diagnosis. Rather, the goal is, over time, after you've taken five to ten tests and read your computer-generated report, to find common themes. Take time to think about these themes. How have they impacted your career? Think especially about where you found success. How have the positive traits helped you to achieve your goal or to feel successful and happy when doing your job?

Self-reports can be excellent predictors of your behavior. One problem is how you appear to yourself. How many of us are willing to admit we are too often duplicitous or lack moral values? We want to appear socially desirable, even to ourselves. Thus we have a tendency not to confront or challenge our own behavior. But when people do challenge it, they don't diminish themselves. When they honestly try to grow, they make progress in maturation.

Personality quizzes are a form of introspection. The asking of certain questions serves as a guide. The test is designed to help you understand how you believe you react to stress, how assertive you are, and so forth. These self-reports are converted into a score, and the score is used to predict behavior. The only question is the degree of correlation to outward behavior, not whether there is a correlation. These measures are self-reported. You think about and decide upon your own evaluation of yourself. Thus, these more naturally predict behavior under conscious control.

For example, if I score low on emotional stability, I would have a tendency to react when my beliefs are confronted. If I score high on altruism, I would be drawn to causes that promote philanthropy. If I score high on competitiveness, I would enjoy being in situations in which I was called upon to show measurable results and be ranked against others. If I score high on sociability, I would enjoy a lot of interpersonal contact. And if I score high on suspiciousness, I might enjoy detective work or being an investigative reporter.

THE ENEMY'S MIRROR

To understand yourself better, look at people you dislike. So often when we take a dislike to somebody it's because their personality traits unconsciously remind you of your own weaknesses. As one scheming executive told me: "When two cannibals meet on a path, they assume each wants to eat the other. Thus, they immediately become defensive and aggressive." The aggressive person dislikes the agreeable person, and agreeable people immediately feel aversion to forceful people. Those with hidden agendas dislike open and straightforward types. Dealing effectively with people we dislike teaches patience and compassion.

> → Try this: Think about the people you instinctively feel uncomfortable around. Write about this experience as being an excellent mirror showing where you can grow.

When meeting somebody for the first time, all types of sensory impressions flood into conscious awareness. More importantly, impressions also flood into unconscious awareness. They combine and culminate in an overall reaction. Do you like or dislike this person? Your impression goes beyond five senses. You combine emotional reaction, physical reaction, and visual impression into a "gestalt" or whole.

We probably dislike only a few people we meet in life. Most of us don't have a Richard Nixon "enemies list." (If you have to write down all the people you consider enemies, you have too many enemies.) As long as people stay in their space and you in yours, all is well. Many personality types must coexist to make leadership successful. It's important you understand your hot buttons when it comes to disliking people. What we desire to correct in others often is what we seek to correct in ourselves.

> *Everything that irritates us about others can lead us to a better understanding of ourselves.*
> —Carl Jung

→ Whom do you genuinely dislike?
→ What about this individual, specifically, do you dislike?
→ Does this person activate a weakness of yours?

CONTEMPLATE THE PATTERN OF MISTAKES AND SUCCESSES IN LIFE

Going through disappointing times, failure, or loss isn't fun, but it does lead to self-awareness. After a divorce, moving out of the house and getting a small apartment where you have a lot of time alone to learn, think, reflect, and grow is illuminating. Dealing with pain and disappointment isn't enjoyable. Nevertheless, more is learned from these events than from having fun at the beach. It seems we think and feel deeply when in psychic pain. Why this is true is a mystery. But I know from my life that this has been the case. To have become a deeper man or woman is the privilege of those who have suffered.

A useful exercise in learning to bounce back from stress and disappointment is reflecting on life patterns. By your forties, you see patterns recur in life. These patterns are subtle. They're always there. One positive aspect of aging is the ability to reflect on patterns and decide whether you like what you see.

We learn throughout our lives. Sometimes it's trial and error. We see a situation and go for it without doing our homework and fail. That's good in the long run; it teaches humility. Maybe we are lucky and get to understand the virtue of patience. People often will say they wish they had more patience. Secretly, to themselves, they are proud to be a "type A." To them, a lack of patience signifies how productive or forceful they are. With insight comes lessened anxiety. You are aware of what sets you off. You can build up coping mechanisms and choose how to react, truly having more control over the outcomes in your life.

→ Where did you back down in the face of strong opposition?
→ Is there a pattern in what causes you to stress out?
→ Are there patterns in what causes you not to be as successful as you wish?
→ What are the subtle patterns in your life?
→ What are the obvious patterns to your life?

Do not go where the path may lead; go instead where there is no path and leave a trail.

—Ralph Waldo Emerson

Another reward of aging is the ability to look back and see consequences. By seeing consequences, we become aware of the poor and good decisions we've made. Life is about making decisions, seeing consequences, and then growing and improving. Reflect and listen to your heart. We've never met a person yet— and we've assessed and coached thousands—that didn't have a great deal to learn and a great deal of potential growth.

When we examine our lives by looking back, we find "truths" we held dear to our hearts that turned out false. Our belief was an illusion. At the time, we treated our belief as fact. For example, we might have admired a person. We wanted to follow him and be a part of his success and future. Yet, over time, we see that the charismatic figure contains seeds of dishonesty and manipulation. He lacks loyalty. We get tricked and taken advantage of.

We are resentful when people turn out not to be who we thought. Everyone has examples of people that initially impressed but ultimately disappointed. We become angry with them. Then we are angry with ourselves for having been duped. We might have gotten angry with friends and family for telling us things we don't want to hear about the people we put our faith in. We are forced to admit, sometimes sheepishly, they were right and we were wrong. We all know truth is in the eye of the beholder. With maturity, a person is guided by the facts of the situation, not by what they want to believe.

→ What have been your life lessons?
→ Reflecting back, what personality traits do you have that are double-edged swords—that are helpful but have hurt, too?
→ How have you changed over the last ten years?
→ What did you used to think was important? Are the same things still important?
→ How would you like to be different ten years from now?

When one door of happiness closes, another opens; but often we look so long at the closed door that we do not see the one which has opened for us.

—Helen Keller

CONSIDER THE TURNING POINTS OF YOUR LIFE

→ What specific choices did you make?
→ Were some turning points coincidences?
→ What coincidences moved you forward?
→ Do you sense a pattern to your coincidences?

EXAMINE YOUR BELIEFS

Beliefs shape self-identity and management of stress and disappointment. Consider what circumstances cemented your beliefs. How did your upbringing contribute to forming your opinions? Your beliefs should not be misinterpreted to say you have knowledge; *beliefs are not knowledge*. Good leaders understand this. That is why they want and demand facts. They want beliefs, too, but want facts that justify their beliefs.

→ I believe power . . .
→ I believe money . . .
→ I think people should . . .
→ I think competition . . .
→ I would like to achieve . . .
→ I want employees to describe me as . . .

Knowing yourself means you understand what makes you whole as a person. You know your values and core strengths. When a good decision is made, it intuitively resonates. You're heading in the right direction.

Self-knowledge means you understand weaknesses. Over time you learn where you too often make mistakes. You see patterns and gaps in your thinking. You are more able to navigate around problem areas. You bring in smart people to help think through issues and improve judgment.

→ What I am most passionate about in life is . . .
→ Being honest, my limitations include . . .
→ Over my lifetime, I have refined my skills in these areas: . . .
→ My core values are . . .
→ Some of the things I don't want anybody to know about me include . . .

The more you are like yourself, the less you are like anyone else, which makes you unique.

—Walt Disney

4

Becoming the Leader

Speaking as a senior executive, behavioral scientist, and business coach, I believe there are two behaviors an effective leader must excel at:

1. Holding deep conversations within him- or herself.
2. Holding deep conversations with others.

People who are successful in leadership generally have a pretty solid grasp of how smart they are and how they typically deal with different types of tasks and challenges. Hence, they stick with a leadership style that is natural and instinctive.

There is all sorts of advice on how to be a good executive. Every bookstore carries many books describing leadership. It is sometimes interesting to read about leaders, successful entrepreneurs, and so on, but it's very hard to imitate their panache, personality, and attributes. Most people slip back to their natural behavior over time unless they receive ongoing coaching or are very committed.

Let's look at Steve Jobs, the CEO of Apple. He is described as brilliant, narcissistic, a perfectionist, intuitive, a micromanager, exhibiting messianic zeal, mercurial, and egomaniacal. Some of these attributes don't sound very nice, do they? Not traits many of us would want to imitate, yet Jobs is considered the Henry Ford of our generation. By all accounts, he is a highly successful leader. Fortune magazine named him "CEO of the Decade" in 2009.

Let's talk about Barack Obama. He has been described as a confident conciliator, self-assured, ambitious, gracious, considerate, and benevolent. He has an affable charm with an ability to bring opposing viewpoints together to solve problems. He is known for turning problems into "teaching" moments. All of these are excellent attributes. Taking these characteristics into your own leadership personality would probably be a pretty good thing.

But reading about qualities rarely imbues you with them. And that is the purpose of becoming your own business coach: The way to develop yourself as a leader is to understand who *you* really are and to speak from *your* heart. The same is true for your leadership style—you must ultimately stay with your natural personality. It is our goal to bring out the potential in your leadership skills through helping you understand more deeply who you are.

Your personal quest to be a better executive or entrepreneur should ideally be just that—to be a better executive or entrepreneur. A philosopher could argue that to be a better person is enough of a reason to read this and similar books and articles. But this reason, although rational, is not as worthy a reason to lift others to their positive potential. Taking people to the next level makes you, and them, a better person. For isn't that the essence of leadership—to elevate people to manifest their contributions?

➜ Why do you want to improve as a leader?

Don't approach this question superficially. A thoughtful answer will help to fulfill your dreams, because it forms the foundation of your personal vision. Your answer's depth gives energy and commitment to ride out the inevitable challenges that lie ahead.

> *God helps those who help themselves.*
> —Benjamin Franklin

Personality is genetic. It's also composed of psychological events we've long forgotten. Hidden deep in the unconscious, these memories affect our leadership because they shape our personalities. These forgotten memories may be the reason we don't have the inner confidence necessary to improve on our own, even though we'd love to. So often, we need the insights of outsiders and their counsel to improve. Even Tiger Woods has a coach

> *Consider how hard it is to change yourself and you'll understand what little chance you have of trying to change others.*
> —Jacob Braude

View your life as a work in progress never to be fully completed. The fun part of life is that there is always room to grow, to get better, to overcome a facet of your personality that is underdeveloped and that you want to change. The more you know about yourself, the more boundaries expand. If we understand ourselves, and go forward using strengths, we'll make significant progress and achieve goals. When we're on the home field playing with strengths, we're confident and play at our highest level.

In any attempt at self-improvement, it is necessary to discover the underlying reasons and blockages that keep you from manifesting your potential. Self-knowledge enhances your life, even if you never rise to be CEO. You'll achieve more satisfying business and life success no matter where your career takes you. When you truly understand yourself, you know your weak and strong points and strategically plan around the weak areas. For example, when you know you're uncomfortable with going into sales, become friends with the sales force. It is through understanding how the selling process works out in the field that you will become a better leader. You do not have to be an outstanding salesperson, but an understanding of what goes into bringing home a deal is invaluable. A leader obviously doesn't have to have expertise in all functional areas, but needs to understand the basics and appreciate how each discipline adds to the company's strategic direction.

Of all human resources, the most precious is the desire to improve.
　　　　　　　　　　　　　　　　　　　　—Anonymous

Be open-minded when you read and work through the upcoming exercises. Don't be judgmental. Don't chastise yourself because you're not living up to self-imposed standards. This retards growth. Besides, you don't need to overcome all your weaknesses. The secret is recognizing them and taking them into consideration when you're laying out your game plan.

You don't always have to be right, either. There is freedom when you realize your perceptions and actions may contain flaws. You are not going to lose self-esteem when you recognize an error in judgment or action. Be a little humble. Learn from everyone you meet. You'd be surprised at the wisdom and insight a taxi driver, a janitor, or a vendor has on occasion. They could reflect the wisdom you need at that exact moment in time. The smart executive learns from many people if she's open-minded to receiving information and ideas.

Have you ever learned something interesting from an unexpected source or person you wouldn't normally think you would?

Leaders who are in touch with the common qualities of humanity and express them in a meaningful way can provide great insights. Even your children or dog can teach you lessons. My children remind me to keep life in perspective; they tell me exactly how they perceive me, without garnishment, which is helpful. My dog Skippy teaches me that loyalty, love, being petted, and being happy in the present are what life is all about.

> *The only normal people are the ones you don't know very well.*
> —Alfred Adler

Business is business is business. In fact, leadership is 80 percent the same from position to position in industry. But each leadership role needs a special passion. You must possess a passion that causes you to reverberate with excitement, a calling or spark that makes you come alive. This passion allows you to work hard, yet not feel tired. To find this one, resonant note within you is the key to contentment and satisfaction. Discover yours.

→ What don't you like about your present leadership style or skill set?
→ What's interfering with your ability to unlock your leadership potential?

All human beings are propelled by one basic drive: the desire to receive. People wish to receive food, love, safety, security, belonging, self-esteem, self-fulfillment, and success. The deeper question people don't ask is: What is it I wish to receive? Often people accept too simplistic an answer, or a response of "I don't know what I want." If you don't know what you want, life is vague and directionless. Yet too many people find themselves in this state because they don't want to go through the mental gymnastics of self-clarification. This is a life error. Some people don't want to decide what they want because it gives them a face-saving way to explain their lack of commitment. After all, if you don't try, you don't fail. Right?

→ What is it you wish to receive from the universe?

When you take these personality quizzes and write in your answers, it is a form of introspection. You're being guided by the asking of certain questions. Since these measures are self-reported (you thought about and decided upon your own evaluation of yourself), they more naturally predict your behavior that is under your conscious control. Note that the short tests in *Becoming Your Own Business Coach* come with a disclaimer: Because they are specially written to flow with the themes of the book, we haven't validated them against the general population. In our opinion, it is more important to view these as experiential in relationship to "you." There is no other person who will see the scores or leanings one way or another. So you can be perfectly honest and open. The goal is simple: the improvement of self-knowledge.

LEADERSHIP PROFILE

This profile is designed to evaluate your entrepreneurial leadership. When you take the profile, the reference point is that you're the senior officer of a company with a team of eight people directly reporting to you. Subsequent layers are under them.

1. By giving others in the company authority, the leader loses control.
   a. Strongly agree—The leader calls the shots, period. That's why he's the leader.
   b. Moderately agree—For the most part, the leader needs to call the shots.
   c. Disagree—This is what holds down most companies and people from ever developing.
2. Your company is working on a proposal. One employee comes up with a good angle. Meanwhile, you have simultaneously developed an alternative strategy that is just as good. Which solution do you go with?
   a. Mine—I'm the boss, it is my division, my concept, and I know what we need to do to sell deals.
   b. Hers—I need to demonstrate I listen and am flexible.
   c. Ours—I'm willing to bet two heads are better than one and a combination will be the best.
3. You finally delegate a task you historically have done. What defines the performance standards for the person who fulfills the job?
   a. Your old standards—you did the job, you ought to know how it's done; stick with a standard that's proven to work.
   b. Let the employee do the job with some supervision and come up with his own standards.
   c. Eighty percent of what you did and how you did it, and 20 percent how the employee thinks it ought to be done.

4. When the person to whom you delegated the job makes an error, what do you do?
   a. Take back the job—it has to be done right.
   b. Correct the error without telling the employee because you don't want to squash productivity.
   c. Sit with the person and together correct the mistake and relate the mistake to the vision.

5. Your company's culture should be:
   a. An honest day's work for an honest day's pay.
   b. Professional.
   c. Fervent believers who are on a mission.

6. When you get together at the end of a day for a company meeting:
   a. You feel it would be a leadership mistake to share your opinions, ideas, feelings, and information. Your job is to see employees' feelings be put out on the table.
   b. You generally prefer not to get too involved, even though in principle you don't mind sharing your opinions, ideas, feelings, and information.
   c. You readily share your opinions, ideas, feelings, and information to help the group discussion and use it as an opportunity to shape vision and culture.

7. When you are leading a company discussion:
   a. You leave people who don't participate alone. If they don't want to, why should you force them?
   b. You usually actively invite others to take part in the discussion.
   c. You always actively invite others to take part in the discussion. You realize everyone has a contribution.

8. When someone in your company shares a good idea, you:
   a. Feel that person is invading your role as the leader.
   b. Feel happy for the person because they feel involved.
   c. Let him or her know you value the contribution and, if it's a good one, give them some responsibility for its implementation.

9. Which of the following statements do you most believe?
   a. Highest efficiency is achieved when people have strong oversight.
   b. Highest efficiency is achieved when people have a very complete job description.
   c. Highest efficiency is achieved when people feel connected to a vision.

10. To what degree do you agree with the following statement: "The most important thing people can do is to fulfill their job description."

a. Strongly agree—If everybody fulfilled their job description, we'd get the work out best.

b. Strongly disagree—People have to have freedom.

c. Somewhat agree—A job description is a good starting point, but you don't want to impose too narrow a path. That's for companies that don't fully engage their people.

11. To what degree do you believe it is relevant that group members are aware of the organization's goals?

a. Mostly beside the point—get the job done.

b. Somewhat relevant.

c. Critical.

12. When working toward a goal:

a. You focus on the details.

b. You focus on the big picture.

c. Both are critical, but the big picture is the aspect to progress toward.

13. Do you have a clear vision of where your organization is headed?

a. The vision changes so much that I need to concentrate on the task at hand.

b. We'll cross the vision road later. We have a few years to go before that.

c. Definitely.

14. How important is it for you to create a personal connection with the members of your company?

a. Not critical.

b. Somewhat important.

c. Critical.

15. How do you feel about differences of opinion among individuals within your company?

a. Differences quickly turn into animosity. Put a stop to it right away.

b. They are generally healthy.

c. Differences of opinion are best used for creative problem solving and original thinking.

16. What does it take for people to follow you?

a. The more incentives, the more people follow.

b. A combination of incentives and recognition.

c. People naturally follow me because of my vision and enthusiasm.

17. I think planning:

a. Is irrelevant.

  b. Should be done on a formal yearly basis.
  c. Is ongoing and adaptive to changing conditions.

Count each (a) answer as one point, each (b) as two points, and each (c) as three points. How high was your score?

- 48–43: You have a leadership style and perspective that does well in an entrepreneurial company.
- 33–42: Average; you might find it frustrating to wear so many hats and uncomfortable with leadership that demands flexibility, quickness, and delegation.
- Below 33: Stick with a more process- or procedure-oriented role until you understand and feel comfortable running an entrepreneurial division.

HEAD VERSUS HEART

Executives tend to think and reason in one of two ways. One is an intellectual or objective approach. The other is through the heart—an emotional and intuitive approach. This dichotomy has been noted throughout history. For example, examine the writings of Thomas Hobbes and John Locke, early sixteenth-century philosophers. Hobbes comes from the head; Locke from the heart. Other dualities exist that take on these characteristics, including: introvert/extrovert, qualitative/quantitative, rational/intuitive, right brain/left brain, math/humanities.

It is relatively easy to spot a heart-driven leader from a head-driven one—much like observing a calm person compared to a nervous person. Interpersonal difficulties arise in the "fit." When the manager is heart and the subordinate is head or vice versa, one type never really understands the other. Each can be frustrating to the other.

1. My coworkers view me as an outwardly animated person.
   a. Yes
   b. No
2. My office is well organized.
   a. No
   b. Yes
3. I prefer reading:
   a. Imaginative perspectives of business marketing.
   b. Realistic, factual accounts of case studies.

4. If I am in charge of a project, I need to have the details carefully worked out.
   a. No
   b. Yes
5. When I am in a team meeting, I am careful about making up my mind too quickly.
   a. No
   b. Yes
6. I share feelings and emotions with coworkers and my boss:
   a. Openly.
   b. When necessary.
7. Before I put forth a strong opinion or position in a group meeting, I like to wait and get the facts and details straight.
   a. No
   b. Yes
8. When turning a set of bolts from a weird angle, I get confused about which way to turn them to loosen or tighten.
   a. Yes
   b. No
9. I would rather:
   a. Write a best-selling book about creative business decision making.
   b. Win the Nobel Prize for economics.
10. I am detail oriented and remember numbers well.
    a. No
    b. Yes
11. When in a business conference I like:
    a. To be open and say things spontaneously.
    b. To get thoughts well organized first.
12. When I give a business presentation, I am entertaining.
    a. Yes
    b. No
13. I am the sort of manager that goes strictly by the book.
    a. No
    b. Yes
14. For employees, it is more important to:
    a. Have a team-oriented attitude.
    b. Get their jobs done correctly.

Count each (a) response as a "heart" and each (b) response as a "head" indication. How many a's and how many b's did you mark? Which way do you lean, or is your score balanced?

There is wisdom of the head, and wisdom of the heart.
—Charles Dickens

Heart Leaders

Heart-driven executives are often extroverted, interpersonally effective, socially skilled, and spontaneous. Open, emotional, and emotionally reactive, they make decisions impulsively to escape anxiety. Patience is usually not one of their virtues. They view work subjectively and make visceral judgments and decisions. They "roll with the punches." The heart executive is stimulated and motivated by ideals; objective, quantitative facts are secondary.

The following are some characteristics of a heart-driven leader. Check the ones that describe you. Especially note any you want to improve on.

- ☐ Holds open discussions where interruptions, spontaneity, and different opinions are heard.
- ☐ Holds meetings to resolve challenges, not just for information.
- ☐ Attentive to feelings; emotionally in touch with people.
- ☐ Intervenes to resolve conflict.
- ☐ Puts out "fires"; very responsive to the environment.
- ☐ In touch with a large range and type of employees across many levels.
- ☐ Adapts to the present.
- ☐ Demonstrates emotions/moods.
- ☐ Changeable.
- ☐ Tends not to pause for reflection.
- ☐ Can be too concerned with image.
- ☐ Needs public praise; depends on approval.
- ☐ "Drops" names.
- ☐ Struggles to be objective.
- ☐ "Feels" situations rather than thinking about them.
- ☐ Reveals much of the self through behavior.
- ☐ Can react too emotionally; acts first, thinks later.
- ☐ Needs appreciation.
- ☐ Wants to be popular.
- ☐ Feels safe from gnawing self-doubt only when convincing others.
- ☐ Wants to make a good impression.
- ☐ Outgoing, candid, trusting, and adaptable; quickly forms attachments.
- ☐ Can "roll with the punches" and make quick, spontaneous decisions.

☐ By nature, wants to get close to the customer.
☐ Has a coach or educator management style.

Total = 25. How many did you check?

Head Leaders

Head leaders are intellectual. Generally, they express what they think, not what they feel. Head leaders are less comfortable with feelings. Often they make it to the executive suite via their financial expertise, constant focus on the bottom line, intellectual prowess, quantitative analysis, and ability to make good decisions.

Intellectual executives concentrate and tune out distractions to highlight the important tasks. They organize and prioritize objectives, isolating and focusing on the most worthwhile endeavors. However, a tendency to hyper-collect—obsessively collecting more and more information instead of making a decision—can lead to being overly conservative.

The following are some characteristics of a head-driven executive. Check the ones that describe you, and make special note of any you want to improve on.

☐ Is objective.
☐ Is rational.
☐ Is not easily influenced.
☐ Strongly tends to believe blindly in own thoughts and consider them to be objective.
☐ Is consistent.
☐ Has a hard time describing feelings.
☐ Tends to be aloof and overly dependent on a tight circle of advisors.
☐ Does not tell others about what he is doing or why, just presents the final result.
☐ Tends to prefer impersonal communication.
☐ Is cautious.
☐ Investigates; likes to collect information.
☐ Can appear calm even when very tense.
☐ Kindles less flame in others, more in herself.
☐ Tends to rule out the opinions of others.
☐ Holds a grudge.
☐ Desires to "win" intellectually.
☐ Wants to, and worries about, appearing intelligent
☐ Does not easily give praise.
☐ Can become defensive when disagreed with.

☐ Dislikes taking social risks.
☐ Feels uncomfortable with self-disclosure.
☐ Does not show enthusiasm.
☐ Does not like soft-skills management training.
☐ Has a high need for power.
☐ Likes empiricism; inherently skeptical.

Total = 25. How many did you check?

Fusing Head and Heart Styles

Fusing the head and heart into a balanced whole makes for an objective and emotionally sensitive person. The rational, quantitative "head" approach and the intuitive "heart" approach are both useful and valid—but all the more so when fused together. Quantification is an external validation. Feelings are an internal validation. Both orientations have strengths and weaknesses; both are partially correct. Our version of truth is flawed; you filter truth through your personality.

Maturity allows executives to get out of their comfort zones. Intellectual types learn to be more emotionally motivating. Heart types learn to be more analytical. Fusion is the middle ground. Superior executives succeed by balancing objectivity and emotions. A kind heart is kept in place by a wise head. Good ideas contain feelings and thoughts. Evolved managers do not squelch ideas by demanding facts, but neither do they buy into ideas by being emotionally swayed.

You will do well to study your opposite. Gain clarity as to what you do not and will never deeply connect with. Reduce the downside—and increase the upside potential—of either style.

➜ How do you need to develop a better balance between your head and heart?

Balancing Techniques for the Head Manager

Go on sales calls. Open your eyes and ears. Your understanding of business may not be as strong as you perceive.

See the lighter side of yourself. Do not take your ideas too seriously. Poke fun at yourself in a permissive atmosphere. Give yourself the go-ahead to be open with your feelings.

Head managers are inherently critical. Work to overcome being judgmental. Try not to "win" interpersonal dialogues by withholding information or boxing the other person into a corner.

Deliberately respond on a positive feeling level. Give compliments.

Watch a dialogue and describe what you saw using affective adjectives. Increase your feeling vocabulary: "agreeable," "caring," "considerate," "good-humored," "receptive," "understanding"—or, for unpleasant affective states, "degraded," "confused," "skeptical," "touchy," "insecure," "overwhelmed," "worried." Foster emotional awareness by watching and describing what the other person is feeling—this increases empathy.

Balancing Techniques for the Heart Manager

Try not to be so tuned in to the energies of others.

Focus on internal awareness and harness the power of mental discipline. Develop contemplation, detail orientation, thought, and reflection. Keenly investigate aspects of business situations before making decisions. Explore issues, be patient, lay groundwork.

Use the scientific method of decision making:

- Try to make decisions intellectually, cognitively, and rationally to eliminate personal bias. This is done by trying to compute the amount of uncertainty compared to what is known to be true.
- Decide what is or is not part of the problem. Gather sufficient information. Identify key dimensions of the problem.
- Assess which factors can be controlled and which cannot.
- Identify the priorities of the preferred solution.

What the human mind can conceive and believe, it can accomplish.

—David Sarnoff

STAYING RESILIENT

You don't ascend to leadership to be comfortable. You go into leadership because you want to achieve through the achievements of others. You'll go through some lonely times when the whole reality of the senior leadership experience sets in. You begin to encounter obstacles, many psychological. It can test your limits. But these times help you learn. Too many people focus on frustrations, often excessively and usually pointlessly. An important lesson is that every day you'll get up and face challenges, obstacles, and frustrations—the question is, are you going to look at problems as opportunities? Look for solutions; don't focus on emotions.

Remember the adage that God (or the universe) never puts you into a situation you can't handle. The more you realize and believe this statement, the more your fear dissipates. The fact is—and the older you get, the more you understand this—you can lose everything through an unfortunate accident or bad luck. Maybe this is scary or humbling. Yet you can't live your life through fear. You have to get up and go to work every day to solve problems no matter what you do. Fear drains you of natural vitality. It is the biggest detriment there is to thinking big. If you don't overcome unproductive fear, you're not going to rise to your potential.

When a disruptive event happens, we can be paralyzed. If we overcome the cloud of anxiety and visualize where we ultimately want to be, our path becomes clearer. When we are paralyzed, we can't see the whole picture. These feelings are effects, not causes—something makes you feel the way you do. Through introspection, try to determine why you feel emotionally paralyzed.

Ironically, the scenarios that make us the most uncomfortable are the things we need to most embrace and work on. All of us have fears. By not addressing them, we inhibit our potential. Uncertainty is powerful. It can keep you frozen and prevent you from being proactive. Naturally, when you think about rising to the top, you're going to experience uncertainty. This is especially true when you're starting your first P&L or sales job because there are so many "firsts" day after day. You're going to experience occasional twinges of doubt about your ability to make things happen. This is natural. You're a fool if you don't occasionally admit and own these feelings. If you don't, it means you're not looking at the downside risk and the negative things that can possibly happen.

➔ Who was the best executive you've ever known?
➔ What qualities did he or she possess?
➔ What qualities would you like to more emulate?

Doubt is the brother of shame.
—Erik Erikson

HOW FORCEFUL ARE YOU?

1. When my boss does something that bothers me,
   a. I usually let it go.
   b. It depends on the circumstances.
   c. I usually speak up.
2. In a situation where I'm in charge,

   a. I don't like to give people directions.
   b. I sometimes feel comfortable giving people directions.
   c. I like to provide directions.
3. People think of me as more:
   a. Cooperative.
   b. In between cooperative and aggressive.
   c. Aggressive.
4. If my boss or clients are doing something I think is wrong, I tell them my opinion.
   a. Rarely
   b. Sometimes
   c. Often
5. If being polite and pleasant doesn't work, I will be tough and sharp with employees.
   a. Rarely
   b. Sometimes
   c. Often
6. If a client and I were joint-venturing a project and I didn't agree with his ideas, I'd:
   a. Always allow him to make the decisions.
   b. Perhaps offer a suggestion.
   c. Let him know I thought my way was best.
7. When customers, clients, or coworkers don't see things my way, I usually can talk them into buying my ideas or solutions.
   a. Not often
   b. Sometimes
   c. Almost always
8. If I notice my boss's line of reasoning is wrong, I:
   a. Let it pass.
   b. Perhaps offer my thinking.
   c. Directly point it out.
9. I enjoy the competitiveness part of business.
   a. No
   b. Sometimes
   c. Yes
10. I let other people decide what to do.
   a. Often
   b. Sometimes
   c. Rarely
11. I don't really mind if other people take charge of things.
   a. True
   b. Sometimes
   c. False

12. When conversation lags at an economic mixer, I pick things up by talking the most.
    a. False
    b. In between
    c. True

13. I usually take charge of things when I'm sitting on a work committee.
    a. False
    b. Sometimes
    c. True

14. I try to strongly influence the senior leadership team.
    a. False
    b. Sometimes
    c. True

Count each (a) answer as zero points, each (b) as one point, and each (c) as two points. The higher your score, the more forceful you tend to be:

- 0–7: Not forceful
- 8–12: Moderately forceful
- 13–21: Above average in forcefulness
- 22–28: Very forceful

Strongly dominant executives can get what they want— but pay a price. In business, smart, mean, tough people can do well under the right set of circumstances. But when you're so controlling you won't allow people to inject their judgment or ideas into your team, the team tends to stagnate over the long run. It is not bad to be competitive or controlling in the right situation. Knowing when and where these behaviors are called for is the key.

OBSTACLES

Your biggest challenge in becoming an inspiring leader is psychological—getting through mental challenges and recognizing and overcoming emotional fears to become your ideal self.

Obstacles take us to our next level of business development. For example, if you ever played sports, you appreciated a great match or game against a great opponent. There is nothing like going up against an evenly matched team and having both teams play their hearts out. Victory is much sweeter under these circumstances. And, even when you lose, there is a certain majestic quality to the encounter.

Metaphorically, think of your career as your star athlete; now think of the business environment and climate—the challenges and aggravations—as the opponent. You're going to win matches, but your opponent is, too. Your opponent's goal is to get you to give up because of the obstacles. Your opponent raises the bar every time you have any type of success. When you lose, pick yourself back up again. Losing builds character and an appreciation for triumph in business just like it does in sports.

One fundamental reason managers want to be leaders is that it increases happiness. Recall that thought when the alligators are coming for you. Leadership fulfills a psychological need for people who have the need for power. Of course, we want to select leaders whose need for power isn't for self-aggrandizement, but for organizational achievement. You need to do the work to be successful. Dreaming and hoping doesn't create success. It is only through action and dedication that things happen.

OVERCOMING FEAR

Fear doesn't exist until we become aware of it, reinforce it, and give in to it. Fear creates barriers. Some fears are healthy. The scary reality of the marketplace causes you to be proactive. Fear of losing sales, or even your job, will motivate you to make ten key customer calls a day. An excellent reaction to fear is action.

Sometimes, fear stems from long-forgotten experiences. Fear is programmed into the unconscious. The conscious mind forgets—fear remains. When we are unaware, our fears drive behaviors and decisions.

A useful and relatively easy way to overcome fear is to write out your worries. This supports us in using reason. When you write, be prepared to feel some angst. Get mentally prepared. Say to yourself: "I am prepared to be anxious, to doubt and worry."

➔ What are you afraid of in life?

Think of a time when you were afraid, but your fear was an illusion and there was never really a need to be afraid.

You must do the thing you think you cannot do.
—Eleanor Roosevelt

Once you work through fear, energy is 100 percent focused. You remove apprehensions. When we acknowledge fears, we make a determined, willing effort to say: "OK, life, bring it on. I'm ready to handle whatever comes my way." You've made a decision to hang tough. You're ready mentally to experience what your decision might mean. When you acknowledge blocking fears, you open your consciousness to ideas and energy.

Causes of fear include:

- On a personal level, we are afraid of our complicated lives. When we are successful, we accumulate. Our possessions become oppressive burdens instead of rewards because of the fear we'll lose them.
- You might fear you'll wilt under the pressure of others' expectations.
- You can fear your power will be usurped, or you'll be taken advantage of. Power is part of identity. When power is threatened, identity is threatened.
- Other peoples' fears permeate us. You may have nothing to fear, but by identifying with someone fearful, you learn to be afraid.

Four steps to achievement: Plan purposefully, prepare prayerfully, proceed positively, pursue persistently.

—William A. Ward

OPTIMISM AND POSITIVE THINKING

The linkage of optimism with success is scientifically validated. When given personality tests that measure optimism, successful people score higher. One trait of a successful leader is an overall positive outlook. But executives, particularly sales types, can get themselves in trouble by believing their own "BS" and not consider downside risk.

→ Think through the negative things that can and sometimes do happen. When in life have you been overly optimistic and not taken the downside into account?
→ What happened?
→ What did you learn?

Optimism is needed for your rise to the top, but downplaying risk gets you in trouble. Although looking at things through rose-colored glasses can allay anxiety, thoughtful analysis and sometimes preventative action are warranted. Recognize reality. Weigh risks. Just don't focus on the downside, or else you won't take the decisive action required to get your business going on all cylinders. It's that mature balance between optimism and realism successful people find. Believe that defeat is a temporary setback or challenge. It doesn't knock you down permanently, it just slows you down temporarily.

→ What things could torpedo your career?
→ What concrete steps have you taken to minimize the risk?

Acquaint yourself with positive people and positive situations. Don't surround yourself with unhappy friends who are emotional sponges. Occasionally this means social isolation. Seek those who are on your side of the ball and give energy, not ones who discourage you or tell you that you can't make it happen or achieve your goal—even your mother, if she throws out barbs such as "Dan, wouldn't it be better if you kept your present job instead of looking for such a big opportunity?" While these comments seem innocuous, even kindly meant, peeling back the layers reveals that what is meant is that you're not good enough.

Don't get sucked in. Be polite. Change the subject. Try not to let relatives or close friends pull your strings or let doubt enter your consciousness. You'll be confronted with negative people when you are trying to change behavior.

If you have a good business friend, talk openly with her about your dreams. Sometimes spouses are good in this role, sometimes not. It depends. Perhaps it is unfair and unrealistic to expect your spouse to consistently see situations dispassionately. Attachments, expectations, desires, fears, and needs intrude.

If your spouse has trepidation about you going into commissioned sales, you don't need to have your fears bounced back to you amplified. Somewhere in your dialogue is the fear you won't be successful. The family's lifestyle might suffer. Maybe you're reasonably self-confident, but if you listen to well-intentioned people who project fears onto you, it limits your ability to move forward.

We find it far easier to persist in approaching life when surrounded by others who are empathetic and support us, rather than siphoning off our precious energy. You may be surrounded by those who give the message that you're not good enough and that you can't compete, people who point out all the pitfalls and obstacles. If you find yourself smothered, maintain even more vigilance over your own thinking. Devote plenty of effort to changing your circumstances and fending off the negative people, even if it means changing jobs.

> *Think you can or think you can't, either way you'll be right.*
> —Henry Ford

Optimism doesn't mean avoiding warning signals or denying unpleasantness. Optimism paired with psychological "tough-mindedness" is a great combination. This means being tough to psychological and physical pain. OK, your back hurts—what's the next question? Yeah, you feel like crap today, so what? This deemphasizing of pain, difficulty, and frustration tends to set people apart. Life's negatives can be acknowledged, but it does little good to fixate upon them. You have a headache—pop a few aspirins, breathe deeply, and go out and bring in a sale. When you close a big deal, I will venture to say that your headache will magically disappear. Top executives have little time for dwelling on misery. There is a client who needs to be visited!

You can accept the reality of a situation, and then imagine the situation in a way that leads to action and problem resolution. Simply tough it out. Taking the day off because you're stressed out or feeling sick doesn't cut it. (Obviously use reasonable judgment; if you are truly sick—and we all get under the weather despite our best intentions—take time off.)

If something goes badly, focus on how you will do better. Adapt and change your thinking. Pessimists think through oppositional filters. An anonymous author defined a pessimist as "one who feels bad when he feels good for fear he'll feel worse when he feels better."

Pessimists point out the obstacles, the downside, the risk, the misfortune. They have a little cloud of negativism over their head. They worry unconstructively. If things begin to pick up and the future looks sunny, they will point out how it can't last. And yes, there is often an element of truth in the belief—but the element isn't the whole truth. Pessimists see the business environment crowded with waiting traps. People are out to get them. Customers are out to screw them. Employees take advantage.

Recognize traps, for they *are* out there. There is an optimistic vision when you lay down fear that is (always) attached to the ego. Focus on the constructive, upbeat aspects of business life. The successful executive sees other paths, comes up with more innovative solutions, and internally believes that she can make the strategy happen. You feel motivated when you sense success and movement toward your goal. How can you be continuously motivated if you're pessimistic? Everybody likes to be around positive people who see more good in the world than bad, and praise more often than they blame.

Consider the negative and learn to dig more than one route out of the foxhole. When you develop multiple path solutions you get a feeling of confidence, power, and energy. At least one route, out of the three or four you've created, will work.

→ Think of a situation that is vexing to you. Close your eyes and try to think of three interesting, different, and powerful ways of solving your challenge.

It's important to bring fears out into the open. It's not the darkness you're afraid of, but that which you imagine lurking in the darkness. If you do something that takes risk and fail, it's still worth it. You gain life experience. You learn a lot of interesting lessons about yourself through failure. Achieving success is at the heart of our coaching. But failure is a positive thing, too. You always learn more from failure than success. And if you learn enough, you'll figure out a way to try again.

> *There can be no real freedom without the freedom to fail.*
> —Erich Fromm

You might fear that you truly don't have the prerequisite strengths to pull off your dream. Nobody likes to fail, especially publicly. Nobody wants to go into a new job, have it go south after eight months, and then dribble on a few more months before quitting or getting canned. Not only are you financially hurt, but you're definitely a little more humbled—which might not be a bad thing.

Part of being an optimist is not talking about negatives too much, for our thoughts create our reality. The more we complain, the more we notice all the reasons why we can't be successful. What we focus our energy, time, and commitment on expands. Dwelling on the past, examining events through the lens of fear, moaning about what could have been or should be—all this only causes us to look backward and become disappointed about where we are in life. Long-term successful executives are optimists. Employees want to believe the future is going to be all right. The less we complain, the more our minds have the light that's needed to enlarge our vision.

Try to keep negative thinking or worries to yourself. Employees get jittery when senior executives show excessive displays of concern. Speak of concerns, but phrase them in the language of seeking solutions. Instead of saying, "Man, sales are flatter than a pancake!" try saying, "How do we get sales as robust as we know they could be?"

→ What have you learned from your failures? (I'll bet more than you learned from your successes!)

FAIRNESS

A common complaint: The company—or your life, or whatever—isn't fair. "I deserve a better break!" "I deserve to be treated more equitably!" The usual comeback is: Nobody said life is fair. Since childhood we are constantly told life isn't fair. But is this necessarily accurate?

Life is fairer than we realize. Consider physics: Every action has an equal and opposite reaction. Because it's sometimes difficult to see the cause-and-effect paradigm, we don't recognize that the world *is*, in many cases, fair. Our actions precipitate the energy that comes back upon us. But the time delay between action and reaction sometimes means we don't see the connection. The events that happen take a long time to gestate. Then, when something does happen, it appears to come out of the blue. However, there might have been years of subtle energy behind the event.

People who rise to high levels of success have a track record of success; the past is the best predictor of the future. There is a Darwinian effect in most businesses, and the cream eventually finds its way to the top. When a person is really successful, is life fair? Probably, yes—she earned her success.

People do not exist in our world to provide us a pathway for happiness. When people complain of career unfairness, they fail to see the cause-and-effect relationship. Think of some "unfair" things in your life. Try to understand them, even if you have to go way back in life. Pick up the thread of your personality and behavior that caused this supposed unfairness. We unconsciously bring about events or draw certain energy. Maybe you've been "unfairly" passed over for job promotions. Yet you haven't learned the finer points of interpersonal or listening skills, emotional intelligence qualities that are important for upper management. So even though you've gone back to school, received your MBA, and read all the books on leadership, you've overlooked a critical component.

We see mean, political, ruthless people who get ahead or make a lot of dough on the backs of little people. I've known more than one CEO who is actually proud of being ruthless. Some business-people even believe it's good to be cold-blooded: "Grab all you can because there's not enough to go around." What you don't see is the complete picture—marriages in a constant state of tur-moil, kids experiencing emotional problems, loneliness on a rainy Sunday afternoon because they don't have one true friend.

We too often think of success as a lifestyle. And, while certainly not debating its merits, it's not all life has to offer. A smart, egotis-tical, demanding, obnoxious person *can* get ahead. But life has a scale that is balanced and "fair." What this person achieves at one end, he loses at the other. Our goal is not perfection, which is impossible. But we do want to try to achieve our ideal in all facets of life. Even this isn't attainable, but striving to make us more complete human beings has ramifications in all aspects of our lives. When you grow and become an outstanding executive, one that has deep emotional intelligence, guess what? You are going to be a better parent, spouse, and friend. And you are going to sim-ply be happier.

As consultants to upper management, we are called to counsel successful executives with "big egos." Often these folks have small egos with a big put-on persona layered on for protection. The size of the ego is the difference between your perceptions of what you wish to be rather than what you truly are. They lack real, true, centered, mentally healthy confidence. These types can crash and burn. At some point, a set of incidents occurs that require teamwork, sacrifice, and collective energy . . . and these people can't marshal the resources.

Be careful of success snobbery. You might be in a position to be vengeful and inflict harm or display your newfound power. Watch out for this tendency. Success can breed arrogance. In suc-cess, there's euphoria. There may be a period in your life in which you accelerate and seem to do no wrong. When you begin to develop, you'll become far more perceptive. There will be a period in which you can achieve almost anything you imagine. You're hot. But this is only a part of your development; maintain a grip on reality.

This is actually a dangerous period of self-development. You can lose it all. Don't get overly attached to your position or power, so when it goes away—and it usually does—your self-esteem won't go away with it. Many people who've come before, and who'll come after, will build magnificent careers and achieve more. Keep success in perspective.

ARE YOU "LIMITED"?

Are we limited? Many self-styled gurus espouse the philosophy that our only limits are those we place on ourselves. Yet we know limits exist. Try as I might, I personally can't compete with people who are genetically hard-wired to be great in math or physics. You might study really, really hard, yet be average compared to the group you're competing with. Do these kinds of limits set boundaries on the goals we set in life? *If we focus on our careers emphasizing our strengths, they don't.*

IMPULSIVE DECISION MAKING

Some executives are impulsive to the point of having attention deficit disorder. Sometimes, this is advantageous. They at least get off the dime and get something happening. It can also work to disadvantage because they can drive the car off a cliff. They don't carefully weigh facts. The best thing a marketing- and sales-oriented executive can do is to hire a good CFO or numbers guy to counterbalance his energy. Sure, they're going to butt heads and drive each other crazy. Still, with some mutual respect, each will achieve more than they could singly.

Executives, especially extroverts, have a "do it now" sense of urgency. Some extroverts act with impulsiveness. However, they do act. Regardless of personality orientation, top executives generally get right at a problem. Theory isn't necessarily negated; it's just that the practical is given precedence. As one of my favorite executives told me, "One reason I am successful is I learned to go to the fire." In other words, her behavior is focused and directed. She always does something. When fast-moving executives want to quickly move on a situation, obstacle, or challenge, time spent drives them crazy. Fortunately with experience comes patience. This is the main difference between experienced and inexperienced executives. You're no more creative or inherently smarter as you gain experience, but you see patterns and more of the whole picture.

CFOs, being characteristically bright, believe their opinion is naturally the correct one. If they work for charismatic, entrepreneurial presidents, they can feel that their boss is only a good salesman. The president, in turn, thinks the CFO is a wet blanket who looks at the glass as half full. The CFO is bottom-line oriented; the entrepreneurial president is top-line oriented. Mutually, they fail to grasp that *both* are correct. They need each other. More than they think. Their energies are two sides of the same coin. And, that coin is success.

Leaders exert influence. Be a leader by helping people understand their objectives and priorities. Bring insight. Be naturally curious. The more knowledge you accumulate, the more activated your consciousness. Help your employees define the true nature of their career and job challenges. Empower your employees to feel they will overcome obstacles. Help them feel capable of victory—it's great motivation. When people honestly believe hard work will help them achieve goals, they work hard.

True leaders develop others' potential, bring out talents to the highest levels, and awaken energy through passionate, visible, positive energy. Optimism draws energy. Make your style professionally enthusiastic.

PROACTIVE VERSUS REACTIVE

What does it mean when we say good executives are "proactive" rather than "reactive"? Most of us go about our daily lives reacting to outside influences. Stimuli hit us, and we react. Cold-calling in sales, developing a new territory, or opening up a new line of service is more proactive—you take the initiative to create. Being proactive means expanding markets by opening an office in India or collaborating with a synergistic partner or trying a new business model.

Most employees are reactive. They wait to be told what to do. Then they (usually!) try reasonably hard to do it. Being reactive is psychologically easier. You don't have to think as hard. You don't experience the anxiety that comes with being uncertain. For the most part, our lives are governed by outside influences we aren't aware of. When you're proactive, you bring beneficence into your life because actions tap the highest potential. When you're reactive, somebody else or outside forces dictate your life. You can't be too proactive. The more proactive you are, the greater the chance "out of the blue" miracles will happen. Have a bias for action, a sense of urgency every day. Over time, build a momentum of high-impact energy.

→ Where can you be more proactive in life?

NOT PERFECTION BUT EXCELLENCE

Your goal isn't perfection. When the only acceptable result is perfection, you won't start many initiatives. The quest for perfectionism makes you afraid to try new ideas and approaches. If you ever start, you'll probably quit. You can then tell yourself what you set out to do, and failed at, wasn't your fault. Perfectionism inhibits risk taking.

Perfectionists are often intolerant of themselves and others. Perfection is too often an abstraction. One struggles to define it, and when obtained, it turns out to be an illusion. Hence, the perfectionist feels frustrated and bitter. These are exactly opposite to the emotions needed. Frustration tends to make one vacillate and stay in the same place.

You're going to make your fair share of mistakes. Analyze them. They'll reveal useful information and feedback. Be satisfied to do things well, even only adequately sometimes. Resolve to do it better. Over the long haul, you will beat the perfectionist. You can always hire a perfectionist when you've reached certain goals or levels.

"One man's floor is another man's ceiling." "One man's trash is another man's treasure." Old proverbs and sayings are lessons in perspectives. What is successful in one set of dynamics is viewed as marginal from another viewpoint.

> *To improve is to change. To be perfect is to have changed a lot.*
>
> —Sir Winston Churchill

PERSIST THROUGH "CAUSE-AND-EFFECT"

A critical and not readily apparent reason why people are motivated to work long and hard is that they see a cause-and-effect relationship. Their effort leads to a direct payoff. This is one reason sales appeals to high-achieving people. You knock on X number of doors, you send out Y number of proposals, and you win a percentage of the time. You see, directly, where effort leads to results.

In a large company, it's hard to see this relationship. You're part of long chain of events. There is research into customer needs, analysis of those needs, creation of a production process, sales, accounting, administration, and follow-up to see if the customer actually pays for the goods and services, is satisfied or dissatisfied, and so on. Somewhere along this chain is your job.

When you rise to senior management, you might not do all the jobs. You can usually see the whole. Often, you're the one who designed the process, service, or product. You're the one who puts all the pieces together. Behavioral science points out that when people have a clear view of the effect of their actions, they are more motivated. This is one of the reasons why senior executives have more passion: they see the cause-and-effect chain. Senior executives shape, rather than being shaped by, events.

→ Write three important results of your direct actions.
→ How could you better measure your efforts?
→ How could you help your people link their jobs to the vision?

COUNT ON IT!

Your competitors—and in politically oriented companies, even colleagues—want you to fail. The Darwinism of the market and of corporate America decrees that only the strong survive. You need to be smarter, tougher, and more resilient than the environment. Appreciate the economic fact that the environment is, in the long run, your ally. Once you've cleared hurdles, those same barriers keep competitors from reaching your level. They will encounter the same rejections, difficulties, and travails as you. Will *they* be tough enough?

Even when an unscrupulous fellow employee stabs you in the back, it usually, in the long run, makes you stronger, more agile, and better. Count on being undermined, especially by fellow employees who were in competition for your job. If you got it, and they didn't, you can bet with certainty they will chip away whenever they can. Be aware of this. Don't be politically naive. And, realize that their actions can have the reverse effect. You can look, and be, stronger because you rise above it and are not petty.

People eventually will see maturity and appreciate your behavior. I recently interviewed a very senior executive. He had been employed with his company for twenty-five years. The CEO position is about ready to be offered to him. Many people had come and gone over the years. Former CEOs hired outsiders who were brought in over him. But they eventually didn't cut the mustard. His focus remained on the company and team. In the long run, he won. He always put other people and the company first. Now, he will be the new CEO of a Fortune 100 company. Was he politically naive? Probably, at times. But competency, dedication, and talent eventually won out. This is no guarantee, however, that these qualities will translate into a happy ending. Research indicates that many people who make it to the senior team get there by smooth political skills, not by superior competence.

Taking full and absolute responsibility requires a strong sense of purpose.

How much control do you feel you possess over your life? The more you feel like a victim, the less progress you'll make in your career. You need to see the end game. This helps keep you on the straight and narrow. It keeps you in control and provides the emotional fortitude to steer through tough times.

Another type of responsibility is keeping words and actions consistent with values. Being responsible requires that temporary needs and distractions take a backseat to mature focus. As we make our daily choices, the question needs to be, "Is what I am now doing the most effective use of my time?" Taking responsibility means persistently working toward what matters. Persistence, resolve, and conscientious dedication are character traits found in all successful persons.

In 2008, Barack Obama defeated John McCain to become our forty-fourth president. The three primary debates were revealing about the character of each man, and about the population who evaluated the debates. If you were a Republican, you likely concluded McCain "won" the debates; if you were a Democrat, you scored Obama as the winner. Obama presented himself in a cool, calm, relaxed way. He showed he was in control of his emotions. McCain was fidgety. Writers and pundits commented about his tics, facial expressions, and angry demeanor. The final opinion was that Obama won all three debates, especially the last one.

Most people watching the debates probably could not tell you the specific policies of each candidate. But they came to a conclusion that one man felt more comfortable in his skin and projected emotional intelligence. They were attracted to Obama's demeanor. Intuitively, they liked him more. When you know yourself, you project confidence. The interpretation is that Obama knows himself and thus has a deep sense of confidence. He knows his abilities and knows when he needs advice.

An old proverb states: "Smooth seas do not make skillful sailors." Business life is about working hard, sometimes failing, hopefully learning, and then getting back on your feet. When you leapfrog over tough lessons, the character-building experiences, the trials and tribulations of growth, don't occur. The foundation for true, enduring success is laid through struggle.

> *Need and struggle are what excite and inspire us.*
> —William James

Tough times, tight markets, obstacles, getting laid off . . . embrace these difficult situations. My mentor once said if you haven't gone through at least three recessions, then you're not a real businessperson. Stresses and strains give us business depth and character. It's the human condition to learn best through tough times.

LEADERSHIP AND EMOTIONAL INTELLIGENCE

Over the past fifteen years, psychology has moved into interpersonal humanism, or the study of how people become successful through dealing with others. The term that seems to have stuck is "emotional intelligence" (EI). Definitions vary, but the unifying theme of all descriptors is that high-EI people understand the emotions and feelings of others, use emotions to influence others, understand the nuances and complications of emotions, and manage their own emotions effectively. AST defines *emotional intelligence* as the ability to deal with one's emotions while sensing, understanding, and effectively applying the power and good judgment of emotions to positively energize a situation. EI is about recognizing and managing your emotions and those of others. It is integrated into our daily life and is considered a legitimate topic of research and discussion.

Self-awareness is a critical component of emotional intelligence. People who are said to have high EI accurately assess their own emotions and how others respond to them. They don't fall into the trap of seeing only what they want to see. They see things as they truly are. Emotionally intelligent people possess social and interpersonal skills. High-EI executives are authentic. For them, social interactions are easy and fulfilling.

This is why highly emotionally intelligent people often do well in occupations and situations that require a lot of contact and persuasion with others. High-EI executives have a reservoir of internal strength and resilience. Thus they overcome difficulties. They control moods. It's easy for them to internally motivate themselves to overcome obstacles to reach goals.

EI emerged as researchers wanted to better understand why the smartest guy in the room was oftentimes not the leader or the person who made the most money. Why do people who score lower on intelligence tests often do better in real life than brighter colleagues? There is clearly another factor at work. EI is a good explanation.

An old adage in the legal world goes something like this. The students who get all A's become judges, the B students become partners, and the C students wind up as managing partners and make the most money. Generally, it is the latter group's EI that allows them to be rainmakers and bring in big clients who generate revenue. Eventually, the leaders of law firms and professional service firms are in general more like high-level account managers. In many cases, EI is as important as cognitive intelligence, especially in businesses where interdependency and teamwork is valued.

From a broad perspective, emotional intelligence comes down to two major domains: dealing with others and dealing with your own emotions. This gets back to an earlier point we made, when we stated that great executives master two skills: holding deep conversations with others and holding deep conversations within.

ATTRIBUTES, QUALITIES, AND CHARACTERISTICS

High-EI people are less fearful of dealing with emotions. An accountant looks at a long spreadsheet filled with numbers with no fear. She's on her home turf; why would she be afraid? People with high EI don't back down when confronted with emotional dynamics. They identify negative feelings without distress. They don't get wrapped up in the emotionality of the moment. They keep egos out.

They understand and deal with their emotions and those of others. High-EI people try to find positive solutions to interpersonal problems and issues. They don't "not talk about it"; they don't avoid the topic of concern. Interpersonal issues are approached with a belief that the predicament can be resolved positively if they articulate what is bothering them and ask the other person to share their feelings. Solutions are mutually explored.

High-EI people quickly recognize what people are feeling. They are skilled at reading body language and tone of voice. They are comfortable allowing themselves to get close with others. Intimacy is established relatively quickly and appropriately. Some vulnerability is provided by them lowering defenses first interpersonally. Objective and genuine support are provided with empathy. A clear mind offers good advice. Being at ease with their own emotions allows them to easily relate.

Ronald Reagan is a good example of high EI. He went from costarring with a chimpanzee in *Bedtime for Bonzo* to being a two-term, successful president. Reagan was not considered by even his allies as possessing high cognitive abilities. But he had terrific interpersonal skills. He trusted his own instincts because he had little garbage in his unconscious that would have clouded his intuitive abilities.

High-EI people share and discuss intimate issues with people, but realize that in most business circumstances, it is inappropriate. High-EI people don't wear emotions on their sleeves. Nor do they talk endlessly about their issues and become energy vampires that suck the life out of a conversation by focusing on their own problems.

High-EI people have the ability to help pick people up when they're down. If you have this ability—and it is a blessing if you do—you might need some alone time to help recharge your batteries. Helping people is intensive and energy giving. When you listen carefully, articulate back to the person what they are experiencing, and describe positives or give encouragement, you demonstrate genuine caring. High-EI people are sensitive to people's emotions and moods, and they listen patiently and pay attention without jumping to conclusions.

High-EI people take time to relax and give themselves time to think. They bounce ideas off colleagues and decide to pursue the idea that makes them most confident in getting results. Rarely do they allow emotions to drive a decision. They try to integrate facts into decisions.

High-EI people regain poise, laugh at themselves, and continue on their way. They quickly calm when angry or upset. After a setback, they pull together quickly.

High-EI people don't overly criticize themselves, call themselves losers, berate themselves, and so forth. Why kick yourself more than necessary? What good does it do? Everybody gets down. We do something stupid, or we fail when we think we should have prevailed, and then we berate ourselves too much. Move on. Don't stay down on yourself. It only leads to depression.

High-EI people learn to praise themselves. They don't need others to tell them what a good job they've done. Recognition is a powerful motivator, especially when we value and respect the person who gives us the "atta boy." But they don't constantly need praise for self-esteem.

High-EI people get over their own ego. They don't dwell on negatives. When humiliated (and we all get embarrassed and feel mortified about things we do sometimes), they recognize their emotions, come to grips with them, and move on. They don't reminisce and become ashamed weeks after an incident; sometimes they can even learn to laugh at themselves. They don't feel outraged very often and make the best of a bad situation. They freely admit to mistakes. And, they understand the power of apology.

High-EI people have the ability to share what annoys them and seek solutions. They receive feedback or criticism without defensiveness.

High-EI people understand how to narrow their energies to focus on what needs to get done. They don't set a course without a clear understanding of what they are looking for, so they don't get lost in the weeds.

High-EI people take a breather or timeout (say, once a month or once a quarter) to look within and decide if their present course matches their best thinking on where they want to go. They feel comfortable with themselves and seek time alone to reflect.

When you are accurate in evaluating others, you evaluate yourself more accurately. Those who have a high degree of emotional intelligence also have a correspondingly high ability to introspect. The more accurate our self-knowledge, the more accurate we are in understanding others' personalities. When you have good EI, you more carefully observe behavior, both others' and your own.

You probably have experienced people whose interpretation of reality is significantly off. This can range from those who just don't seem to get it to a full-blown schizophrenic whose grip on reality is tenuous at best. *When people continuously misperceive their environment, they misperceive the causes of their own behavior.* Paranoid people constantly see threats even when there are none. Depressed people see the negative in situations that hold no negativity. People with anger management issues see conflict everywhere that "forces" them to react.

If a person has severe deficiencies in his understanding of others' motives and underlying reasons for their behavior—that is, he hasn't got a clue—then it makes sense he lacks the ability to understand or develop an internal theory on *why* he behaves as he does. A good part of our self-knowledge stems from self-interpretation of our actions and feelings. Observe and interpret your own behavior. Through the development of an internal dialogue, you predict and control behavior.

If you want to become more emotionally intelligent, a good place to start is with introspection and fostering a better understanding of your own motives for behaving in a certain way. To look inward, you need to look outward. We look outward for most of our lives and indeed form much of what we believe about ourselves based upon how we respond to the outside world.

→ Describe yourself to yourself.

Now pretend you are describing yourself to another person who hasn't met you. Isn't it fundamentally the same?

Most of us want to talk our lives over with a trusted advisor to get "outside" observation. We want to share thoughts, feelings, and experiences to validate that what we are thinking about ourselves is accurate. The outside advisor may know you well, but does not have the understanding of the emotions you experience. If a set of advisors validates your thoughts and conclusions, it opens up your ability to initiate action. In other words, if several close friends tell you to do what you believe you ought to do, you do it.

I had a friend call me for my opinion. He thought he should get aggressive in interviewing for a coveted job in Arizona. He thought he should contact the CEO and ask if he could fly, at his own expense, to interview a second time for the opportunity. He felt his candidacy was slipping away. Thinking he was number two, he wanted to do something to change the landscape. I told him yes, do it. It would demonstrate his motivation to earn the job. That was all he needed. He immediately made the call. He showed good emotional intelligence by checking with somebody he valued (me) to see if my recommendations rang true with his introspection. (He didn't get the job, by the way. But at least he had no regrets.)

Often, it is helpful to recognize your emotional state. Then objectively, almost in a third-party way, say to yourself, "I am experiencing anxiety," "I am feeling trapped," or "I am feeling dejected." If you feel heart palpitations or your breathing is shallow, your introspective labeling correlates with your physiological state of affairs. By taking the time to step back and cognitively label the feeling, you begin to gain mastery over your condition.

There is a concept called "theory of mind" that describes innate skills such as responding to the content of other minds. As human beings, we see (roughly) the same thing as other people. If people hear a great politician speak, most (at least if they are from the same party) observe and feel similar emotions. When the CEO speaks of a hoped-for vision and competitive threats, she assumes employees form a mental image that is similar from employee to employee. If "everybody is on the same page," communication flows quickly and effectively.

SHARING RECOGNITION

Is your desire for success really the desire to receive for yourself? To move the business or your work team to the highest level, you need to overcome the desire to achieve for your own pocketbook and ego; you need to share. It's an important concept that can't be overstated—a big problem that, if not properly understood, limits growth. If your basic orientation is "The more you give, the less you have," you'll limit growth.

Actually, the opposite philosophy is true. This desire to line your own pockets with money or to achieve ego recognition is at times fatal. At the time of this writing, America is beginning to undergo a shift in consciousness because of the financial melt-down of 2008–2009. Perspective, acceptance, personal responsibility, and enjoying the simple things of life are becoming the new currency. Greed, self-indulgence, and possessiveness are no longer the definition of happiness. All of this is more good than bad from a mental health perspective.

To hit the big time *and stay there*, one must share the pie of recognition. Basic, positive sharing so both parties gain is a metaphysical principle that is so true and right on the mark in business.

When you get to the point where you have a great employee who can take over your job, give her a piece of your responsibility. This frees you to open the next phase of the growth of the department. If you keep the decision making, recognition, and bonus money to yourself, you'll eventually lose the most talented of your employees. What you'll have left are underlings doing your bidding. But all they want is a steady paycheck and to leave at 5:00—hardly the type of people needed to move the enterprise forward in tough times.

At the very least, create an environment where employees grow, make a good salary, and take care of their families, a place where they feel good about themselves. When you create this environment, you infuse your setting with a sense of ethics and values.

The great executives that managed to create huge industries certainly had the desire to get rich or to do well. They wanted the lifestyle, big home, and toys. But at some point, material possessions are tapped out. You can only be in one room at a time no matter how big your house is. You can only wear so many clothes, only have so many cars. There is, at some point, for really successful executives, a fundamental value they are trying to establish beyond lifestyle. They begin to layer their organization not with hired help, but with people who are smarter than they are. The business really moves to the next level. The company dramatically increases in value.

Think big. But contemplate how you'll use your success to do more than buy houses, cars, boats, airplanes, and toys. Career goals should include material success, but also spiritual and social success. With increasing triumph, there should be a concomitant sense of giving something back, which completes the circle. Most executives who have made a lot of money tend to give away a lot—only to find that giving, for some reason, opens the door for more money to flow in. Most successful people share wealth. Be prepared to contribute and give back. Be appreciative of your position in life. Reflect on how lucky you are. When you are successful, be sensitive to people. Share success. You'll expand even more.

Employees are motivated when they "receive." In order for people to be motivated to take action on your behalf, they must sense they will receive something in return. Realize that if you are going to get anywhere, you must receive energy outside of your own abilities. When you achieve what it is you set out to do, spread it around and away from you. Create more space for new, even more powerful energy to come into your work team or division. This is an important part of being successful: knowing when to give, and when to receive.

BUILDING ALLIANCES: THAT FAMILY FEELING

The high-achieving executive doesn't think twice about making nonroutine requests. He expects commitment that requires effort, initiative, and persistence from his team. If the team leader creates the euphoria of a "family feeling," employees usually deliver. It is here that a delicate balance of coercion, legitimate purposes, and genuine sharing must occur. When people perceive the executive is out for himself and he unscrupulously uses people, the family feeling ends. Employees begin to look for ways to even the relationship. They will take advantage of the situation whenever they can, often through passive compliance or passive aggression. The positive dynamics of feeling tight-knit are mirror imaged; advantages become magnified disadvantages.

Most executives typically establish a special bond with a small "in-group." This usually includes a loyal administrative assistant everybody knows they have to get along with. This small number of people is given greater influence, benefits, and power in return for demonstrated loyalty and commitment. This in-group was usually there in the beginning and has squatter's rights. Some are brought in by the executive from past relationships. There is nothing inherently wrong with this, but naturally there's some resentment felt by the rest of the company.

You may form special relationships with employees that are based primarily upon loyalty, not necessarily competence. It is not unusual to outgrow these relationships for one reason or another. When you do outgrow these relationships, check yourself to see it's not because of fickleness or lack of long-term loyalty on your part, which it can be. We have seen examples of leaders who only let some people into their inner circle when they need them to accomplish the mission. These leaders have a fundamental fear of being found out for the unscrupulous person they really are. So, they rotate people out of their life about every three years.

Many executives have more than their fair share of self-centeredness. After all, they want to rise to the top, chart their own destiny, and take responsibility for doing so. But there is a reverse side of these seemingly admirable qualities, including the tendency to use people, selfishness, greediness, and manipulation. Don't kid yourself; you may have more of these tendencies than you want to believe.

Though different people bring different capacities into the workplace, treat everyone equally. Respect and kindness (not softness) shouldn't vary. It's a way to instill a family feeling, which is really fun. Perhaps you run a small company and will never be able to compete with big companies in terms of the usual "motivators." You need to rely more on psychological motivators.

> *A great man shows his greatness by the way he treats little men.*
>
> —Thomas Carlyle

Don't judge people by your standards. Most people don't have your intellect or ambition. But some people have more, so be humble. We all make mistakes and miscalculations in our career that usually take us down a peg or two. Everyone has strengths and purpose on this Earth—as do you. People who work for you, for the most part, want to do a good job and be respected for doing it. Don't take away their dignity just because you are the means to their paycheck.

All human beings want basically the same thing at the root level. Freud said it was to love and to work—good relationships and financial success. Don't forget that people want from their job the same things you want. It is our core nature to want to be happy and fulfilled.

Keep pressing on all fronts. Develop a kind of spiritual connection with what you do. When you build your career and go about your job from this connection, work is easier and fulfilling. You know you have a great relationship with your customers and employees when it becomes increasingly interconnected; that is, both parties are sharing and receiving from the relationship. There is a unity and harmony. People work through problems because the relationship makes a union, a whole, like any positive human dynamic.

Work should fulfill psychological needs. These needs include achievement, affiliation, autonomy, nurturance, order, and understanding. If none of these needs is met—if there is no sense of freedom, innovativeness, creativity, or challenge—the workforce becomes demoralized and experiences high turnover. It's not rewarding. Employees show up only for a paycheck. Humans have an inherent urge to create harmony and excellence. People want to perform well. A picture frame at an angle causes a psychological need to straighten the picture. As a leader, tap into this genetic desire people possess to strive toward excellence.

CHARISMATIC EXECUTIVES: THE SHARKS

Be prepared to meet "sharks." The more successful you are, the more they'll be showing up at your door. Shark executives are energetic, conceited, and ostentatious. They don't share. Their goals are accumulating money and power, and unfortunately they can achieve both.

Sharks have self-destructive tendencies such as drinking, violent tempers, and sexual perversions, especially in private. They may have terrified wives and emotionally unhealthy kids. They lack a conscience. They lack true class. Yet they may sound sincere; some are excellent salespeople.

Learn to spot these sharks. They have no true friends. After all, in their book, other people are there to be used for personal gain, nothing else. Like sharks, they stay on the hunt.

You probably have witnessed executives who leapfrog over people and are almost—or in some cases, truly are—sociopathic. Some people understand how to manipulate their environment. They take advantage of opportunities, "manage up," and cover their tracks beautifully. They know just the inflection point of bending but not breaking the rules; they are "legally correct."

It is maddening to watch sharks succeed; however, over a lifetime there is a cause-and-effect paradigm. Whatever energies you send out, both good and bad, are given back to you in one form or another. Sometimes the time between the cause and the effect masks the relationship, but it is virtually always there. In other words, we do seem to get what's coming to us, in one way or another. I have seen sociopaths in business. Look for the person who job-hops every three years, just before it is brought to light that he isn't worth the paper his inflated resume is printed on.

Sociopaths have superficial charm. They are manipulative and out for themselves. People are used as victims. Think of Bernard Madoff's $50 billion Ponzi scheme. Madoff was a financier who duped people out of their life savings, yet showed no remorse. And, in a sense, he couldn't show remorse. He is sociopathic. By definition, sociopaths have no sense of guilt. They have no real love for others. What they want is power over others. They believe that they are genetically superior and entitled to certain rights of success. They lie easily. And they believe their own lies so much that they can even pass a lie detector. They have no conscience, no sense of remorse. They will be nice to people if they see them as accomplices. But when the person is no longer useful, out the door they go.

Sociopaths are the opposite of genuine. They have an incapacity for caring. Verbal outbursts, callousness, and rage are all part of the syndrome. They usually have a secretive, paranoid quality. In more recent descriptions, their condition is referred to as antisocial personality disorder. There are an estimated two million psychopaths in the United States.

You will be taken advantage of by a sociopath/psychopath at some point in your life. The more you understand your weaknesses, the better prepared you are to deal with this deviant. Why? Because sociopaths size up people quickly and effectively and will play to your weaknesses. As a leader, if you hire one of these types (and they generally will go into some type of sales role), you will know it by their ability to always have an excuse ready to con you into believing that a big deal is about to get closed.

There are executives who have upbeat, charismatic personalities with a dark side, due to their lack of maturity or self-centeredness. The ruthless leader takes advantage or is unsupportive when the going gets tough. People who need personal power and enjoy influencing groups strive for upper-echelon positions. When the need for power is coupled with immaturity and high intelligence, there is a real problem. These leaders are in the game for personal aggrandizement and dominion over others. They blame, cover up mistakes, hog recognition, grab money, and run a company into the ground, bailing just before being exposed. When an executive lacks integrity, look for job-hopping. This will be disguised as wanting to get ahead. Because of our mobile society, it's easier to camouflage a lack of integrity.

When the leader's emotional maturity is low, she's impulsive. Undulating emotions set up a chaotic environment. Usually she doesn't resist hedonistic temptations and is unable to delay gratification. Mood swings or angry outbursts eventually drive off quality people. She's left with second-string employees. No one wants to work for a ruthless person.

→ Have you ever met a shark?
→ Did he initially fool you with his charisma?
→ What was the telltale sign that caused you to see through him?

Sharks sometimes use an "inspirational" speaking style. They make appeals to the grand vision of where the company is headed, the purpose it serves for society, why the company is different, and how the employees can be part of something greater than they alone could achieve. Followers perceive that the leader possesses a divinely inspired mission that is unique and bigger than life.

We've seen charismatic cult leaders manipulate their followers to have absolute trust in the correctness of their beliefs, unquestioning acceptance, and willing obedience. The movement may grow, but the movement is connected only to the one leader.

People have a human need to attach themselves to visions they perceive are greater than they are. In this sense, they become more powerful for being part of the vision. When these types of leaders treat the employee well, take time to sit and talk one on one, and listen, the employee can be tremendously rewarded and inspired.

> *Our chief want is someone who will inspire us to be what we know we could be.*
> —Ralph Waldo Emerson

Most executives occasionally resort to the use of coercion or manipulation to accomplish objectives. But one can't do that often. If these tactics are used in lieu of real power, eventually the bill comes due.

Here's an example. You promise a key employee a promotion or big bonus if she will help at the beginning of a turnaround effort. You may have selective memory, but the person you made the promise to doesn't. She will remember vividly. Promises of future rewards motivate people. Be prepared to follow through with your commitment.

If you are thinking about joining a company with a charismatic founder, assess why others left. There will be an unmistakable pattern. Does the leader promise all kinds of things but never deliver? There is always a line of eager people desperately hoping for a career move. The shark will sucker them in, use them, and spit them out. Don't let it be you! A mild degree of paranoia helps you discern the difference between a good, sound story and a good-sounding story.

Call yourself on any sharklike behavior you're indulging in. Realize when you are using manipulation and admit it to yourself when you do. If you pride yourself on your charismatic personality, realize that paranoia may lie beneath your gregarious nature.

I've seen executives achieve what they set out to do through persuasion and inspirational appeals. When they first join a company in a new position, they get people to do things for them through charm and promises. At some point, the leader begins to believe in his greatness and infallibility. He uses the same tactics over and over again on the same people. But employees aren't stupid (though some are exceptionally vulnerable). The charismatic executive comes to thinks too highly of himself, believing that, if it weren't for him, people wouldn't have jobs. He becomes arrogant, manipulative, and domineering. There are no effective avenues for appeals, independent reviews, or new ideas. There is only his opinion.

There is no doubt that successful senior executives are clever, ambitious, and driven—much more so than the average person on the street. But just because you're the smartest person in the company doesn't give you the right to abuse anybody. Just because your career has taken off doesn't give the inherent right to intimidate people. That is too common, unfortunately, with people who achieve a high level of success quickly. They begin to believe they're superior. Their ego gets hard to bear. Their thinking is, "Look how well I'm doing compared to everyone around me or who works for me."

BRIDGING YOUR ACTUAL SELF AND YOUR IDEAL SELF

Effective leadership, regardless of the business situation, is a synthesis of creativity, critical thinking, practical intelligence to mold ideas into reality, and maturity to understand how to balance the needs of all the stakeholders and the future of the entity.

No one is born a leader. Arrive at your own belief as to your ability to evolve your skills. If you regard traits and abilities as fixed by genetics, you are less likely to change than if you view traits as malleable to development.

Leadership has never been more important. But one issue that confounds us when developing ourselves as leaders is lack of agreement on what makes for an effective leader. If you ask a Republican if President George W. Bush was an effective leader, chances are you will get an affirmative answer. If you asked a Democrat the same question, you would get disapproval. Who is correct? Because of this lack of agreement, we have not undertaken to create any type of grand theory of leadership all could agree on. The popular press and biographies of great leaders make it seem as if certain individuals through karma, genetics, and timing are transformational in their effect on the world. (Behavioral genetics research has found evidence that 30 to 50 percent of the variance for psychological traits is due to genetic differences between people, so it appears some aspects of leadership just might have an inheritability component.)

At one time, leadership was thought to be a general personal set of traits that were independent of the context or environment in which the leadership was played out. This was a heroic and more charismatic view of leadership in which great men rose to the occasion. Over time, researchers determined that the specific situation in which people found themselves was just as important as the person. As one Air Force pilot told me, "John Glenn was a fine man, but he happened to be in the right place at the right time to make history; there were others just as qualified as he."

Some situations require a more autocratic leader; others need a more consultative, participative leader. At our consulting firm, we try to understand the business situation, the key issues or goals that need to be achieved to gain success, and what specific competencies are (supposedly) required, and then we try to match the right person to those variables. Our effort is to fit a leader's abilities and style to the specific behavioral requirements of the position.

Certain leadership traits are considered universal. Leaders need to be persistent, for example, because the blockages to success are usually more serious than originally conceived. Tolerance for ambiguity is needed, too. Although the vision might originally be clear, the vision adapts and molds over time to what the customer is willing and able to buy and to the continually altering business environment. Self-confidence is always important, because there is plenty of criticism and negative feedback.

There is a host of people wanting to see you fail, some within your own company so they can have the satisfaction of believing their way was correct. There must be a relentless energy and drive, as well. The hours are extensive, the obstacles many.

Over the long haul, there must be integrity. Integrity is vital to keep and nurture a top senior management team. They have a good view of who you really are as a leader. The CEO must be above reproach in behavior and values. An effective leader needs to be an optimist. She must believe that if the team pulls together, communicates well, and keeps its eyes on the prize, the goals are under its control; the company can and will come out a winner. There also must be an achievement motivation or internal drive. Often there is little extrinsic reinforcement and congratulation when you arrive at the top, particularly when the organization is struggling. Of course, the CEO and senior team must possess high intellect, which is one trait that is almost universally agreed upon.

There are many different ways a leader can behave and still achieve the goals the board, stakeholders, and others agree on. Excellent leaders know their style and what circumstances call for one type of leadership over another. For example, if a company is failing and a tough-minded, even authoritarian, turnaround is needed, the leader needs to have decisive skills and a certain callousness to the individual human condition compared to the group need. At this point, structure, timelines, and specific financial hurdles are imperative. Yet, if one is running a creative ad agency that has a good client list, an effective leader needs to be engaging and have a fun, professionally friendly, collaborative environment. You can see how one leader would fail in the other dynamic. This helps explain why a CEO candidate who has enjoyed much leadership success can come into a new environment and "fail." Timing and context are incredibly important.

We assume the leader is able to change the organization's culture by replacing the top management team, which he or she usually does within eighteen months after arriving on the job. More often than not, the culture is more deeply embedded because the previous leaders selected, nurtured, and reinforced the style and behaviors most like them. In other words, over time, the organization takes on a certain character because of self-selection and leaders selecting people who remind them of themselves. Additionally, the actual market can often severely hamper or help a leader. For example, if office space in downtown Chicago is at a premium and a new CEO is brought in to run a real estate firm with a core expertise in leasing, guess what? The new

CEO is going to be a winner. If he just doesn't screw things up, he will look like a hero.

In technology firms, sometimes a new CEO is brought in just as a product is almost ready to be launched. The product is then introduced to the market, and sales take off. The CEO is credited with tremendous leadership. In fact, even if he had done nothing, sales would have skyrocketed.

The point here is that situations affect and shape how leaders lead. The situation (context) itself often determines the level of success rather than the personality traits, knowledge, and skills of the leader. And the quality of the "followers" is every bit as important. Remember the phrase "It's hard to soar with eagles when you're working with turkeys"? Well, it's true. It is the followers that play a dynamic role in reinforcing or punishing the leader's behaviors; they empower the leader or undermine his efforts.

→ Why would people follow me?
→ How effective am I as a follower?

Another question that is worth asking:

→ How do your personal attributes interact with your corporate culture and organizational dynamics; that is, are you a good fit for the opportunity you find yourself in?

In this book, we have not tried to distinguish effective leaders from ineffective leaders. Leaders may have extroversion, charisma, a strong work ethic, and high intellect, but can "drink their own bathwater" and fall victim to their own (usually increasingly) egomaniacal, obsessive self-preoccupation. Indeed, the study of failure in leadership is just as instructive as studying successful leaders. This gets back to one of the themes in the book: learning from your mistakes and failures so they won't happen again.

THE NATURE OF CORPORATIONS

Human capital is replacing financial capital as a corporation's most important asset. Although cash is and always will be a significant driver of business—and the one driver that is most accessible to measurement—leadership, management, professional skills, and sales talent are the real underlying assets.

In the beginning of the industrial age, employees were considered a form of a machine. They did a series of sequential duties that resulted in a product. Employees were grateful for a job. They complied with dehumanizing structure, boring tasks, and unsafe, unclean conditions. They didn't have any choice. And, all things considered, conditions were superior to laboring on a farm. They were willing to deal with the abysmal environment because they earned enough to enable their families to have a better lifestyle. Even today, lower- and mid-level employees will put up with quite a lot of boredom and authoritarian bosses, depending on the job market. When times are tough and unemployment is a problem, authoritarianism slips back into the management style. Those supervisors and managers who are predisposed to it sense they can get away with petty outbursts and controlling behavior to fulfill ego needs for power and dominance.

Corporations too often suppress creativity. Some companies and employers aren't interested in your personal growth or in your opinion as to how things could be done better, even though they should be and often claim to be. Virtually all companies post values on their website proclaiming a "people orientation."

Large companies require the completion of tasks. The human resources department conducts job analyses on various positions. From these, job descriptions are written. These descriptions are required in legal proceedings to prove competence or incompetence when an employee is let go. Employees are expected to operate within their job description. That's what they are supposedly paid to do. In most corporate work settings, employees are controlled: what time they arrive, what time they eat, what time they leave, their performance appraisal—all symbolize control.

Corporations, even the best ones out there, demand traditionalism and acceptance of the status quo. In these settings, individual desire is subjugated to the team. You're expected to walk a straight line and mind your manners. But as you've no doubt already discovered, you can follow all the rules, play the game adroitly, and still get screwed. Some companies might espouse how they value "intrapreneurship," that is, entrepreneurial spirit within the corporate setting. But when I interview employees, they tell me for the most part this so-called cutting-edge culture doesn't exist, except in the minds of the executives who attended the latest management course.

So many corporate handbooks and policy manuals are fossilized do's and don'ts that deny freedom of thought and action to the individual employee. Don't take my cynicism too strongly; in today's litigious world, companies need to cover their bases. They have a fiduciary obligation to do so. Companies try to protect themselves against the steady, nonstop lawsuits from certain employees who want to take advantage of our legal system. And there are always cheering lawyers who want to take advantage, too. Because of this legitimate fear of unwarranted lawsuits, there is a defensive, bunker mindset of forms, regulations, manuals, and posters. The result is that creativity, spontaneity, and risk-taking take a back seat to appearances, political correctness, and rigid policies.

This lack of creativity and rigid structure within large corporations is what drives many people to appreciate smaller and mid-size companies, especially when they can be on the senior team. Large companies, as part of their strategy, buy small companies because they are more cutting-edge and innovative. Be thankful for large, cumbersome dinosaurs, for these make easy targets. Fly in under their radar, grab market share, and then sell them back their own market. Isn't America great?

In a large corporation, most employees aren't part of the decision-making process, except occasionally when it relates to some aspect of their job. In a smaller company, they get to influence everything, depending on the personality of the founder or owner. When a business is small, a family feeling motivates employees. People feel they're players on the same team and that they have close relationships and a spirit of commonality. Employees can easily see how their work relates to the mission of the enterprise.

Being able to understand how your work is connected to the whole is important. Studies indicate that when people see how their efforts contribute to the complete product cycle, it's more satisfactory than just doing a piece of the work. Employees, when they join a small company, are looking to have their voice heard, to be in the loop, to be a part of the action. Small dynamic companies are the first to adopt more effective practices and actively search for and create novel approaches. But the small, more entrepreneurial company makes money not on the tried-and-true, widely accepted way—somebody else has already cornered that market. Fresh approaches or a new twist is what drives entrepreneurialism. You're not going to do well if you merely model a successful business; you have to challenge the old way of doing things. This willingness to go for new approaches is entrepreneurial risk-taking, which is calculated risk for rewards.

5

Becoming a Better Team Leader

EVOLUTION OF TEAMWORK

Before the 1980s, corporate America had few quality circles and employee-involvement teams. Organizations were more structured and hierarchical. Command-and-control cultures were the rule. The organization was the parent, the employee the child. As countries began to outproduce America, business realized the value of executives who energize and coordinate people into a team. When team members feel free to contribute, many process improvements are made. The person doing the job day-in and day-out usually has a pretty good idea of the inefficiencies and bottlenecks. Smoothing out all the kinks in a supply chain, for example, can save millions.

If you have been on a team that is firing on all cylinders, the aims and goals of the team move forward at a surprising rate. When you observe these phenomena for the first time, it leaves a lasting impression. You realize the power of positive employee engagement and teamwork.

Today's world demands that leaders establish adult-to-adult relationships with subordinates. Employees are now commonly referred to as partners. The emergent leader, through psychological maturity, realizes that her important role is facilitating the team toward the ideals and objectives of the company. With globalization, the modern leader understands that creating social networks and virtual teams within the company is the key to innovation.

→ Who is the finest team leader you have ever worked for?
→ What qualities does he or she have?
→ What is the one most important thing he or she taught you?
→ Who is the worst team leader you have encountered? Why?

WHY MANAGERS FAIL TO BUILD A TEAM

There are various reasons managers fail to build effective teams. They do not work through others. They alienate subordinates through playing politics, moodiness, and dishonesty. They consistently put their needs ahead of the team's. As a result, employees realize it's an "every man for himself" culture.

Years of research show that leaders who have superior intellect, put their noses to the grindstone, are ambitious, and have deep technical skills from their industry often fail, or are in danger of failing. Why? Because they are arrogant; they allow their egos to become involved in decision making and believe that they are the smartest guy in the room. Even though they may have superior intellect, they just don't seem to understand that within one's own company it's not about winning, it's about teamwork. They can be malicious and come at the issue from a desire to win at all costs, even if it does harm to their fellow workers. Their untrustworthiness lets people know that they can't hold a confidence. Emotionality can derail them because stress causes the executive to lose objectivity and centeredness. Being obsessively bossy and enjoying power inappropriately, thereby drowning out creativity, are other shortfalls. Bottom line? They fail to win the hearts of their people. No leader can lead without followers.

Subordinates and peers are often quite aware of deficiencies and shortcomings in colleagues. We all have flaws. These "darkside" characteristics create emotional distance from all the people that you need to help you. Teamwork becomes untenable.

OFF-SITE MEETINGS ARE IMPORTANT
TEAM BUILDERS

A well-planned and -executed meeting holds benefits that carry on after the event. That's why we believe meetings are not a luxury. And as a leader, or potential leader, it is important that you plan meetings and lead them effectively. This is one highly visible way you can be viewed as a competent executive. Conversely, when you host a poor off-site meeting, your stature is diminished, sometimes irreconcilably so.

Meetings are a necessity in today's hypercompetitive world. There are two overarching reasons why holding meetings can be an excellent investment strategy. These reasons are bringing the unconscious to conscious awareness, and the instillation of corporate culture. These benefits are the real keys to unlocking the growth power of the company. These two factors should not be viewed separately, but are interactive. They result from the entire experience of being in a several-day-long corporate meeting.

Many meeting planners, when asked why off-site meetings are important, respond with answers like, "They communicate important information" or "They improve relationships." While laudatory, we believe deeper, more psychological rationales are at play. It is these profound attributes that are the real reasons why meetings are an important strategy.

CREATIVITY AND THE UNCONSCIOUS

Freud considered the unconscious to be a sentient force of will operating well below the perceptual conscious mind. Creative ideas emanate from the unconscious. For example, how many times have ideas popped into your mind upon awakening, taking a shower, or driving a long stretch of highway that almost hypnotizes you? In essence, your unconscious mind is busy sifting and analyzing information. At the opportune time, when the unconscious has arrived at an insight or conclusion, the thought bursts into your conscious awareness. An "aha" moment occurs.

Off-site meetings create the foundation for this phenomenon. Think about the sequence of a multiple-day off-site retreat. On day 1, participants immerse themselves with data and information. On days 2 and 3, great ideas magically become apparent. This is because the unconscious mind, fueled by an avalanche of corporate communication, has analyzed and explored all the material during the first night. The mind sifts and considers information in relationship to what is already known. The fresh ideas then erupt into the conscious mind upon awakening in the morning of the second and third day. Delphi Techniques or other group problem-solving methods are most effective later on in the meetings. Again, off-site meetings are the best mechanism if your company values creativity and imagination. Wise leaders regard meetings as research and development costs.

At an off-site meeting, people naturally first present their outermost thinking. When asked their opinion, participants respond with what's on their mind. Yet, as your life experience confirms, the more you talk about a topic, the more in-depth your thinking gets. You tap into acumen and wisdom you were not aware of. As you listen and converse, considerations that were swirling around in your unconscious mind become coherent enough to verbalize. Creativity emerges when information is massaged and exchanged by team members. A chain of associations takes place as team members build upon each other's ideas. Contextual cues, body language, and emotional intelligence occur only face to face. And it is these dynamics that produce the valuable insights that push companies ahead.

How often have you said to a colleague, "Let's meet outside the office"? You inherently understand that by changing your environment, the emotional tone will change. This allows you to go deeper in your conversation. It is this emotional depth that well-planned off-site meetings tap into. Altogether different conversations and relationship building occur when people break bread, engage in prolonged eye contact, have the opportunity to study body language, and assimilate a lunch partner's enthusiasm into their own psyche.

Webinars and team meeting conference calls exchange information, but they rarely create the in-depth discussions that produce corporate wisdom. Webinars and phone calls are intellectual. But a great off-site meeting is both intellectual and emotional. This combination of both cognitive and emotional interplay is exhausting. Yet, this fatigue is when an unspoken yet palatable agreement takes place. At some point, people begin to feel freer to express everything that passes through their mind, regardless of where it might lead. Pretenses take a backseat to what is real and honest. This openness contrasts with the usual pattern of communication. Being politically correct and respecting the rankings of power is the corporate norm. But one of the core tasks of an off-site meeting is to face problems squarely and develop solutions.

A several-day meeting gradually allows that which is repressed in the unconscious, or which employees are too intimidated to share, to be brought to the surface and dealt with. Because of the human dynamic of perceived commonality and hierarchical leveling effect through prolonged interaction, true, genuine, and authentic communication starts taking place. Once this happens, people, upon returning to their regular job, understand how to get back to this interpersonal state. The enduring effects of this lowering of defenses to allow genuineness can last for years. If you reflect on your career, you will remember some key associations and relationships that changed your life that were made at an off-site meeting. Bosses became friends, coworkers became comrades, and other departments became partners.

THE DEEPENING OF CULTURE

There is convincing data from the study of primitive human cultures and primates that mankind has always been drawn to groups. These have been characterized by intense, positive, reciprocal interpersonal bonds. Meetings tap into this primal need to bond. Those companies that have a stronger culture differ from their competition in the amount of "groupness." They have a greater sense of solidarity or "*we*-ness." Employees value their company more highly and defend it against internal and external threats. They elevate group norms of positive behavior and participate more in problem solving.

When people become free to express ideas and thoughts, they develop an active and alive feeling. A telling sign that defense barriers are weakening is when inadvertent laughter occurs. The feeling of commonality and esprit de corps takes place. This reveals the feeling of liberation. The cathartic release of the group's energies clears the path for positive action.

Once a company lifts the tightness and tension, the group can have an honest look at issues. They discover the vulnerable spots and what the core competencies of their company truly are. Even if immediate change is difficult, the vision is laid of a future way out of the challenges.

The leader inspires hope, confidence, dedication, and commitment. The instillation and maintenance of these deep psychological conditions is crucial. Employees are always at different points along a continuum in terms of engagement. When employees observe people who are excited about the company's future and their role in it, they become energized. When the leadership team is seen as optimistic, the participants socially model their behavior and attitudes.

People get caught up in the group dynamics of a meeting. When participants observe, "We're all in the same boat," they galvanize toward the ethos and embrace ideals. Human behavior is largely learned observationally and through modeling others. A meeting allows this to occur unlike any other business forum.

Albert Bandura, a social learning theorist, believes in "reciprocal determinism": environment causes behavior, but behavior causes environment. For example, in an off-site sales meeting, the sales team often looks at the top salesperson and visualizes the top producer's quota as within the realm of their own possibilities. As the novice salesperson moves from the periphery of the team to its center, he or she becomes more active and engaged. In the very best of meetings, the new salesperson models and even assumes the role of the high producer. Younger, less-experienced salespeople grow exponentially when exposed over several days' time to the top-tier salespeople. This is the best kind of sales training—observing and emulating.

Business has more anxiety than ever. But meetings with lessons, instruction, and information act as an effective healing agent in the reduction of anxiety. Direct advice from members to each other invariably occurs before, during, and after the meetings take place. Counsel and deeper communication bond participants. Research shows that having people within your company whom you regard as friends reduces turnover and increases morale. There is nothing like a meeting to deepen friendship and reduce apprehension.

In a well-planned meeting, participants both give and receive information, counsel, and emotions. Participants try to honestly hear what other people are saying before jumping in to prove how smart they are. When a pathway is being unveiled, a general consensus builds that is not based on appeasement. If two issues are alike, people try to see the commonalities to create a better process. When participants return from a meeting, they invariably are grateful for having special one-on-ones that impacted their business and personal lives.

→ When have you attended a powerful, motivating off-site meeting?

→ What did the leader do to create these dynamics?

→ Conversely, when have you attended a "lemon" of an off-site meeting?

→ What made it so worthless?

TEAM LEADERSHIP SKILLS

There are several basic, straightforward team leadership skills to use in conducting a team meeting. Conducting effective meetings is important for your career. No doubt you've sat through too many boring, dull meetings that were used primarily for communication, not client-centered strategy, problem solving, and brainstorming. These are the real reasons why meetings are critical.

Here are some tips:

1. When holding a team meeting, state problems in such a way that the team does not become defensive but instead approaches issues constructively. Make statements in terms of common objectives. Try not to state or imply a preference for one idea or suggestion. Avoid preconceived ideas, especially when you want suggestions. For example, try saying, "Our goal is to drive our top line," instead of "The sales

team is weak." Or "We need to create great processes to allow information to flow," instead of "Many of you are bottlenecks."

2. Try not to make long, preliminary speeches—simply supply the facts as you see them.
3. Draw people out so all team members participate. Help reluctant individuals realize that their ideas are wanted and needed. Prevent talkative individuals from dominating the discussion—but don't reject them.
4. Develop the ability to wait out pauses. This skill is one of the most difficult capabilities to perfect. Pauses trap the leader into continuing to talk, calling on people, asking leading questions, and suggesting ideas. The same pause that makes the leader participate too much should instead be used to cause the team members to enter the discussion. Next time a silence comes up in a meeting, wait it out. It can be difficult, but team members quickly learn that you are not going to always bail them out psychologically.
5. Prepare beforehand. Develop open-ended questions that stimulate problem-solving behavior. Questions from the leader cause all team members to think about the same thing at the same time. If the question is a good one, it will direct exploration along fruitful lines. Good questions prevent thinking from reverting to areas where failure is repeatedly experienced.
6. Summarize as the need arises. This skill moves discussions along and shows leadership. It indicates progress. After summarizing, state the problem in a new form. Point out differences within the team. Restate accurately the ideas and feelings expressed in a more abbreviated, more pointed, and clearer form than when initially expressed by a team member.

TEAM COHESIVENESS

Teams are interdependent personnel who share responsibility for achieving common goals. Teams are an aggregate of human energy organized and arranged in a form that facilitates the leader's vision. The successful team leader develops cohesion. This is the union of energy that psychologically binds the team.

Cohesiveness is a function of:

- Coordination of effort and work activities
- Clarity of the mission statement (a sense of purpose)
- Clear communication

- Team involvement in problem solving
- Establishment of clear roles
- The right talent for each role
- Development of talent
- Alliances with people outside the team that secure necessary equipment and resources

Now let's do some thinking and reflection.

→ Write a mission statement for your team.
→ Behaviorally, how do you communicate your mission statement to your team?
→ In the past year, when did you bring your team together to solve a problem?

No single theory accounts for how teams fail to become cohesive. Here are several reasons:

- If there is a general tendency of team members to avoid discussing the ongoing process or truth with each other, cohesiveness diminishes.
- If people expect honesty to lead to unpleasant or anxiety-arousing consequences, they keep their mouths shut. Unresolved disputes lead to psychological inertia. Your group will not become a cohesive team if the members do not share honest feelings.
- Progress ceases and problems begin when team members all start agreeing with you. That means no higher-level problem solving is happening.
- Quality teams have as few secrets as possible. Do not have secrets with individuals or with a certain section of your department. Secrets are destructive; they diminish the leader's stature. There is a difference between being confidential and having secrets. Being confidential implies intimacy and trust; being secretive implies privilege and concealment. Members must recognize that secrets or "deals" made between members lead to mistrust and deception and deteriorate the fabric of team unity. Good teams tend to stay away from behind-the-scenes deal making.
- Cohesiveness fails to occur when team members do not really respect each other's knowledge and skill but merely pretend they do. Egotistical people often lack respect for other members of the team, particularly when they consider themselves intellectually superior. Dominating intellectuals' contributions do not compensate for the subtle deterioration of the team's morale as a result of their superior attitude. To offset

the tactless group member, acknowledge other team members' contributions, virtues, and strengths in front of the dominating member.

I remember so well that, when I first started my career, there was a bright but authoritarian member of the management team. Although he made good points sometimes, he always needed to "win." His tenacious values became a detriment to brainstorming. He quickly judged ideas and emotionally squelched the energy of the team. When he was finally let go, there was a collective sigh of relief. The team demonstratively improved, almost immediately.

→ What secrets do you keep from members of your team? Why?
→ When has a bright, dominant team member robbed your team's creative energy? What did you do?

CHARACTERISTICS OF A COHESIVE TEAM

Some of the characteristics of a cohesive team include:

- *Common goals.* Team members defend the team's purpose, qualities, and products against outside criticism or attack. They are proud of who they are and what they do. The members hold similar beliefs about the goals and purposes of the team.

→ How would your team react if criticized, especially by an outside agitator?
→ Do all the members of your team have the same goal, or are there multiple agendas?

- *Common norms.* Team members want to be accepted by the team, and they will alter behavior accordingly. They value being a part of the team. Members want and desire norms of behavior and live within these norms. Cohesive teams let new people know what norms of behavior are expected.

→ What are the norms of behavior in your company?
→ What are the norms in your department or division?

- *Mutual respect.* Team members should try not to allow their emotions to be displayed negatively within the team setting. It is certainly acceptable to be passionate. However, emotional individual differences are probably best discussed behind closed doors. Members should respect the fact that people come from different races, life experiences, and backgrounds. Show respect for different perspectives. Tolerate unusual people and different ideas. Compromise and admit fault if necessary.

- *Mutual support.* Members want to see others within the team succeed. They are willing to give time and energy to help others fulfill objectives. They show support for members' efforts. Managers get into difficulty when they make goals only for themselves and not for their team. If you want your team to achieve a goal primarily for the expectation of yourself, it drains your team's vitality.

→ How much competition within the team should be encouraged?

→ How much cooperation should be encouraged?

- *Participation.* To maximize goals, people must participate. Successful team members are enthusiastic about the team's goals. They set their goals at the ideal level, not just the satisfactory level. They take pride in individual goals and team goals.
- *Strength in numbers.* Members perceive they can be successful if the team's goals are met. They understand that the chain depends on all its links for strength. They are each one of the links. Everyone is important.
- *Communication.* Members understand the team's objectives and their roles in meeting objectives. All members have strengths. Members use their strengths to advance productivity.

FUNCTIONAL ROLES OF TEAM MEMBERS

Table 1 lists some of the functional roles various team members fulfill.

→ Think about your team and identify the roles of the people who report directly to you. Which persons hold which roles in Table 1? Fill in the right-hand column with their names. How would you classify their personality types?

→ Do you think you give enough recognition?

→ How do you know?

Table 1.
Functional Roles of Team Members

Role	Behavior	Who's This?
Creator	Suggests new ideas and new ways to approach problems	
Clarifier	Seeks to know and clarify the position of other members on issues	
Expert	Offers facts or general rules of thumb about the nature of the business	
Synergizer	Takes ideas and tries to add to them	
Assertor	Asserts authority or superiority; states belief or opinion concerning material or ideas	
Spokesperson	Speaks for how the rest of the company will be affected by decisions	
Supporter	Provides encouragement and support when activities begin to fray; reduces the level of interpersonal tension through humor	
Reinforcer	Provides social recognition and reinforcement to members who work especially hard or effectively	

YOUR PERSONALITY CREATES YOUR TEAM'S CULTURE

The leader's personality infuses the team or division with his or her core competencies and personality. You get long-term employees and stakeholders when you have commonalities that make them friends as well as business colleagues. Like attracts like. When you sparkle, you bring similar personality types around you. Conversely, the more you bring chaos into your company by swings in your personality, the more chaotic-type people will join your team and stay onboard.

John Holland, a career researcher, proposed a theory of occupational types. According to this theory, what people find to be interesting—their natural skills, abilities, values, and motives—cluster into six broad types. We have found that these broad types can also be interpreted as company culture descriptions. When you read the brief descriptions below, find the one that most approximates you and the one your company's culture most reflects.

1. *Realistic* types (for example, engineers) are process oriented, get off the dime, and are focused on the present. Your team

offers solid, steady quality work. The details are taken care of. Customers or stakeholders get value for their dollars.

2. *Investigative* types (scientists) are abstract, original, and independent. Your team likes independent project work that is complicated, challenging, one of a kind. You might rub people the wrong way, but your team will have such great research and in-depth thinking that customers will be back.

3. *Artistic* types (painters, writers, philosophers) are unconventional, nonconforming, and imaginative. You have an open, disorganized, creative culture. Your team creates exclusive products. They help internal and external clients understand products or services in a whole new way. The team often provides internal and external clients with a new vision that opens their eyes to their own core competencies.

4. *Social* types (teachers, clergy, personnel managers) are friendly, idealistic, and altruistic. The team emphasizes listening, caring, and being there in good times and bad. A service-plus attitude is your differentiator.

5. *Enterprising* types (lawyers, politicians) are outgoing, asserting, and manipulative. The team drives sales. This is how the company measures itself.

6. *Conventional* types (accountants, computer programmers) are conforming, practical, traditional, and conservative. Teams are straightforward, steady, on time, and on budget; they are not flashy but the job gets done.

→ Which type is your company's culture?
→ Does your team's culture fit with the company's culture?

Teams can be classified in terms of their primary tasks. For example, realistic and conventional teams will fall in line and perform against a written task list. An authoritative leader who enjoys running the show and directing virtually everything does well. Participatory management does not work as well. Enterprising and social types like participation. They resent lack of involvement or when their opinions are not listened to. Artistic and investigative types like leadership that allows independence and power over their own work.

→ What type do you think you are?
→ What types of people do you manage?
→ How can your leadership style be changed to better accommodate your team's personality makeup?

6

Becoming Your Change Agent

Let's look at reasons why we block our own change initiatives.

It is always challenging to transform yourself all by yourself. The advice and counsel of others, especially those who are brighter or older, is appreciated. How many times in life have your wanted to change a behavior yet struggled to do so? Change is difficult. But we don't give up!

Let's recognize and appreciate your internal psychic forces that push back against your conscious will. Take a longer-term view and push yourself. At some point, determination and motivation win, and you begin to change.

All of us are open to change. And we are all closed to change. It's just the degree of each. Resistance, in and of itself, isn't really bad. Change should come slowly and with reflection. We can't accept many changes at once. We are no different than a company. Some companies can't change because they become complacent, closed, and unreceptive to anything that is not predictable. People are the same way. All the reasons why companies grow stale and dysfunctional are all reasons we do as well.

NO ONE REALITY

When you acknowledge that there is no one reality, you've taken an important step in seeing the bigger picture. Just by briefly reflecting on your life, do you see how your "reality" has changed? Perhaps at one point you saw the world through a set of lenses. You came from a strict religious background, say, and your parents saw the world through a strong, conservative Christian perspective. Naturally you espoused all the beliefs they did. Then, a set of events occurred and now the world looks different. You went to college and took classes that challenged your values and beliefs. You made new acquaintances that provided new perspectives. You had meaningful experiences with someone of a completely different mindset. Suddenly, your old reality is no longer adequate to adjust to your newly discovered information.

→ How has your reality changed?

Recognize that reality is, in certain senses, a projection of values, beliefs, and hopes. Your outlook is valid for you; after all, you never knowingly hold an opinion that you didn't think was true. Ponder this: You are always telling yourself the truth. But one of your friends might think you are "full of it." How many times in life have you looked back and come to the conclusion what you thought was true was false? Besides teaching us humility, we learn not to be so steadfast in our opinions. We understand we can be wrong. We all can be drama queens. But being emotional doesn't change objective facts about a situation. Objectively interpreting facts usually wins.

WINNERS LIKE BEING MEASURED

We are often asked by a client company's board of directors to do executive assessments on several CEO candidates. When a younger (forty-year-old) entrepreneurial candidate was told that the chairman of the board wanted to put him through the assessment process, his response was open and appreciative for the experience. That is often the reaction from exceptional candidates; they want to experience new challenges and find out more about self-improvement. It seems the opposite is true, too; the poorer candidates debate the need for an assessment and believe their track record speaks for itself.

When we agree to coach an executive, we interview him or her in depth on biographical history, successes and failures, disappointment and goals. We put them through a half-day's worth of personality and aptitude tests. After pulling together all the information, we sit down and carefully review results. More often than not, successful people already understand much of the feedback information. After I share the findings, they provide poignant and meaningful examples. When I describe a set of traits or give an explanation as to who they are on a deeper level, they acknowledge and aren't defensive. They are naturally interested and curious in understanding my explanations and insights. Rarely are they outright surprised or defensive. Winners love self-improvement.

AUTHORITARIANS

There is a well-identified group of people, about 25 percent of the population, who believe self-knowledge isn't important. The understanding of self is a concept they don't find appealing. In fact, they feel the opposite. They view the subject as "airy fairy" or mumbo jumbo. These people often are described as having an authoritarian personality.

T. W. Adorno was the first psychologist and personality researcher to formulate the theory of the authoritarian personality. He did this at the end of World War II when he wanted to better understand how basically decent and respectable Germans could have performed such atrocious acts. The basic premise holds that extreme prejudice is a personality trait. The genesis of the condition is linked to people who conform rigidly to cultural norms and values. These people often grew up with a strict father. They internalize the father's values. They repress anger, trauma, and drives. Authoritarians are often mean spirited, yet they would not attribute that quality to themselves; they think they are acting like leaders. They don't usually recognize that their father beat them down psychologically and that they want to beat other people down because of it. Then, because of all the repression or the blocking of these threatening thoughts, they form a strong superego, to use Freud's terminology. A strong superego leads to a moralizing and critical person who has repressed guilt. This guilt is projected onto other people by being judgmental. Authoritarians are condemnatory of any lifestyle, belief, values, or people who don't mirror themselves; they only like people who are like themselves.

Authoritarians tend to like "toughness." They idolize authority and power figures. Authoritarians can be either leaders or followers. The leaders have a high need for personal power; that is, they want power for power's sake, not to use power to advance a higher-order cause. They have a Machiavellian personality in the sense that manipulating others, taking advantage of people, using intimidation, or double-crossing somebody are all OK if these actions allow you to win. Oftentimes, authoritarians make excellent liars and are proud of it. They come at life from a "winners or losers" viewpoint. If there are suckers out there, then those suckers need to be taken advantage of . . . by them.

Authoritarian followers are just as scary. They love to submit to authority. They are usually aggressive, especially to people who report to them or whom they consider of a lower caste. Followers are conventional types who love to be part of a big crowd or movement. The far right-wing radio talk show hosts pull in these listeners. The listeners feel like they are a part of the in-crowd. Their beliefs are reflected back to them. There is certainty. They belong. Often they are extreme, right-wing religious funda-mentalists. They like being a member of a large group of people who all believe the same thing. Self-knowledge for these folks would be very threatening, and they avoid it. (So, some good news here—if you are still reading, you are probably at least somewhat differentiated and not an authoritarian!)

Some people identify so much with a company, sports team, or similar group that they partially lose their own identity and boun-daries. I live in Chicago and am a "Northsider." Now, this may not mean much to the reader, but as everybody in Chicago knows, there are two baseball teams, the Cubs and the White Sox. If you live on the South Side, you are a Sox fan, and if you live on the North Side, you are a Cubs fan. It's just that simple, and there is no deviation from this principle; it is the way it is. Anyway, I go to about five Cubs games a year—not a rabid fan, but enough of one to keep up with the basics of the Cubs' (often disappoint-ing) season. It seems at least one time an outing, I observe several young men who are arguing with a visitor who for some reason is wearing the opposing team's shirt or ball cap. It begins with rib-bing about the other team, then as the alcohol fuels the passions, the young men challenge, swear at, and shout out innuendos at them until a more mature fan steps in and tells them to cool it. Otherwise, there would be more fights than there are.

It intrigues me how people, like the young Cubs fans, can have so little self-regard and self-esteem that they need to infuse the local sports team persona into their own self-perception. When we discuss differentiation, this is what *not* being differentiated is all about! You don't know where you stop and the brand of something else begins. You love the brand, so in order to improve your own self-esteem, you ascribe the brand's identity to your own self. I am not saying one can't be a sports fan. But I am saying that when you use the team to unconsciously prop up your self-esteem, you are on psychologically shaky ground.

RECOGNIZE YOUR LIMITATIONS

Excellent senior executives always aspire to hire people who are smarter, different, or complementary.

If you're closed-minded, that's not necessarily bad. However, you need to understand and admit to yourself you are closed-minded.

Caution people in close proximity that you are. They need to have freedom to throw it back in your face when you act closed-minded. You probably may need to be confronted more often than you think.

The same thing goes with being emotional. This is not to say you shouldn't work on this rather destructive trait. Let people know *you know* you're emotional. They can put your behavior in context and perspective when you lose composure.

Some highly organized leaders are rigid. Rigidity works for them in being administratively strong, procedurally oriented, and dedicated in follow-through. The trait works against them because they run their job and life the same way for twenty years. Change and flexibility are tougher. Rigidity helps create business processes, but it can blind a leader to changes happening in the environment. One weapon a leader has against his competitors is the ability to quickly diagnose problems and make rapid changes. Rigidity can handicap his most important offensive strength.

UNCONSCIOUS DEFENSE MECHANISMS

The concept of the unconscious has been around for as long as man could engage in introspection. From the Indian Vedas to Freud, mankind has always known there was energy within his own mind that caused him to act a certain way, yet he wasn't aware of it. Unconscious motivation is the heart of Freud's psychoanalytic theory, of course. Substantial psychic events take place "below the surface" in the unconscious mind. Many events that used to be conscious become repressed and are then pushed into the unconscious. The repressed events still affect behavior.

We all try to analyze ourselves occasionally. It is relatively easy to reflect on your own behavior and ask yourself what was the true motivation for how you behaved. Even people who believe psychology is mostly mumbo jumbo, or who would never consent to being assigned a coach, occasionally question their own judgment and motivations. We all try to grapple with an occasional incident.

In *Becoming Your Own Business Coach*, we move headlong into ourselves and our motivations on a more sustained basis. The only real issue is whether you agree with the concept that some of your motivations to behave in certain ways are unconscious—that is, the idea that you are not always aware of why you act the way you do. Once you accept this and are sincere in your desire to improve, you will. It's that easy. Every one of us has strengths and weaknesses, and the privacy of our own thoughts and ideas makes it more comfortable to admit these.

The unconscious is studied by outsiders with the use of such tools as the old Rorschach Ink Blot Test or the Thematic Apperception Test. Essentially, the person reports what he or she sees in pictures, or makes up a story on what is seen. The response is then analyzed for themes and repressed material. In skillful hands, such techniques can help people understand themselves. Outside expertise is needed. In this book, we focus more on what you can access and identify on your own. In a broad sense, the book is more about the *access of your conscious awareness*.

If you have tried to break yourself of a bad habit, you realize the power of your unconscious. You know what you *should* do, yet you seem powerless to do it. Forces you cannot identify control your behavior. *Our unconscious is inaccessible to introspection.* But we are fundamentally designed to be able to improve ourselves. Remember, *we are genetically hard-wired to want to improve*.

Inherently, we hold less doubt about our own inner dialogue. We never consciously lie to ourselves. Yet, our unconscious guides our conscious. In other words, we are not fully aware of how we arrive at conclusions; this lack of realization is the culprit behind all the lies we tell ourselves. Mature adults recognize they are responsible for their behavior, despite the fact that sometimes they honestly don't know why they acted the way they did. Think back upon some of your most embarrassingly stupid actions. At the time you did them, they might have made a certain amount of sense. In retrospect, they were stupid.

In the absence, or with lessened impact, of our unconscious on our conscious, we make better judgments. The less our unconscious influences us, the more reliable our decision making.

The unconscious is where our intuition and gut instincts lie. You are not always aware of why you hold certain opinions. You may *think* you are. But more often than not, you think and feel the way you do because of repressed urges, wishes, and conditioning that impacts your thinking. You are totally unaware of this deeper part of your psyche. Thus it is called the "unconscious." This is the part of the mind containing memories, thoughts, feelings, and ideas you are not generally aware of. The unconscious manifests in dreams and dissociated acts.

You reveal the unconscious behaviorally. For example, let's say you have a high ego need for recognition. Because of unconscious motivation, you might misinterpret this need. You believe you're motivated to succeed, but your drive is to fulfill the need for acclaim.

We are not aware of our unconscious wishes or of the forces that drive much of our actions. People often inaccurately explain the causes of their behavior. We sometimes just don't know why we acted the way we did. It is frustrating to have a bad habit you know is bad. You want to stop and change, but seem powerless to do so. The compulsion to act overrides the cognitive reason to not act. Even when you think you correctly identify reasons for actions, you don't know all factors.

People are not aware of the learning and stimuli that metaphysically guide their lives. So, for the most part, people are not aware of the intricacies of their own life history. If we think about it, we give some plausible reasons for our behavior. Acknowledge you are responsible for your actions regardless of any mitigating circumstances.

You bring your unconscious into attitudes and perceptions. For example, some people have issues around self-discipline. They have a high need for pleasure. They can't focus and concentrate. They drink to reduce anxiety. They may attribute their drinking to the belief their skills aren't good enough and they'll be discovered to be incompetent. In actuality, they are competent; their self-analysis is faulty. Yet their destructive behavior continues.

In your ideal state, you want to be the person you know you can be. You may have role models and other important people you admire and want to live up to. You know how frustrating it is to battle inner demons. Your behavior is maladaptive, but you have a hard time changing it. The anxiety that drives the behavior isn't fully recognized. You sense you aren't as happy as you want to be, but you just can't get your arms around the deeper issues. You are not living up to your own standards. You know it. *The difference between the ideal self and your actual self is the level of your distress.*

→ What is a bad habit you can't seem to get rid of?
→ Upon reflection, can you sense any underlying reason that worsens your ability to handle the issue?

Due to not knowing ourselves completely (which we never will), we see events and situations through a lens that is opaque with the grime of our unconscious. Thus, as Anaïs Nin famously said, "We see things not as they are, but as we are." For example, we observe hostility around us when we are by nature hostile. We hear confirmation of our views because we want to hear confirmation. We see politics in the workplace because we are political.

We may think we know ourselves intimately and thoroughly. But in actuality, we often don't. We can be blind to our real selves. Unconscious processes that prevent you from understanding your behavior are called *defense mechanisms*. Defense mechanisms protect our self-esteem and prevent us from knowing ourselves. They are psychological coping strategies used to maintain self-image. We want to think of ourselves in a certain way. We do things and interpret events to conform to our view of reality and of ourselves.

Following are explanations of some well-known defense mechanisms.

Compensation

Portraying yourself in a manner that doesn't accurately reflect the real you, or counterbalances deficiencies, is "compensation." For example, authoritarian, dominating executives may want to appear tough, macho, or important to compensate for inferiority complexes.

Some successful people have insufferable egos that compensate for feelings of inferiority. A large ego filters out the truth. Over the long run, there's a tendency for the big-ego leader to crash and burn. For instance, one time I had dinner with a group of executives. The executive who sponsored the dinner acted polite, but when the event ended, he brusquely walked past the doorman on his way out to his chauffeur-driven limousine while not acknowledging several people with whom he had just dined. I'm sure many of you can remember a time when a senior executive let you know in no uncertain terms that he was top dog and you were an underdog. It happens all day, every day. Just remember, when a man has to show superiority, he is often compensating. True character is shown when a person isn't consciously directing his behavior.

Many of these ego-driven executives don't have the business capability they think they have. The truth of this statement is revealed when they try to establish themselves in another line of business or open up their own firm. They often falter, or the business remains a shadow of what they used to have. A big ego is too susceptible to being swayed by personal likes and dislikes. Decisions are made based on their appeal to the ego. An ego can either propel a person to be great or unravel the chances of success. The secret is balance. Admitting you do have a big ego that drives you is a welcome first step in becoming your own business coach.

Be aware that growth often actually requires overcompensation. When a person lacks assertiveness, for example, he or she is painfully aware of it. A series of assertiveness training classes may initially create abnormal excess—the person may be overly aggressive—before a balance is finally established.

→ Where in life are you compensating?

Denial

Denial is a defense that everybody intuitively understands because everybody has done it, or is doing it, at some point in life. We use the term to describe people who are looking at reality dead in the face yet refuse to see it. "He's in denial." If an employee is in over her head, and her boss likes her, the boss may overlook failures and problems until the issue blows up right in everybody's face. Denial allays anxiety by making it seem like something bad isn't true. The defense involves a pattern of rejecting thoughts, feelings, wishes, needs, or realities you find overly painful.

You could refuse to accept reality because it is too threatening. Or you could argue against an anxiety-provoking stimulus by stating it doesn't exist. Denial is common. To an extent, we all engage in it. Most people caught with their hand in the proverbial cookie jar will say no, their hand *isn't* in the jar. Or they will claim there is strong justification for having their hand in the jar.

In business, when a report is abysmally late, an executive doesn't say his organizational skills are so poor he could not marshal his energies effectively to complete the project. It is psychologically far easier to say there were too many other pressing demands that ate up his time, and thus he was unable to concentrate on getting it completed.

Instant retorts or reactions are one way of not having to deal with an unpleasant truth. Denial becomes a habit or pattern. When you have done it over and over, you don't have to consciously think about it. Thus, denial reduces anxiety.

→ Is there something you say over and over, or do over and over?

Denial stems from the ego's fear that it will be seen for its underlying falseness, or from having to give up or sacrifice an ingrained behavior.

Denial grows stronger and more rigid over time unless confronted and dealt with. An aggressive, sadistic manager will keep on domineering and controlling for as long as she can get away with it. It is fulfilling her needs. To her, she is reasonable, only demanding excellence. To her subordinates, she is a shrew who heaps on stress like lawn clippings on a compost heap . . . and her employees are the heap.

Denial can be a way of telling the truth about a portion of reality as if it were all of reality. For example, an authoritarian manager who hasn't screamed all day can assert, "I don't yell anymore," without acknowledging that that is only since yesterday! Denial blinds people to the cause of their problem. It allows them to pretend their management approach is not destructive. Denial is powerful. Some managers are the last to recognize their disorder.

The abusive manager's denial is painful for those who have to deal with her day to day. It causes frustration. The destructive progression of the department is obvious to everyone except the manager. Sometimes when employees quit, or the results of a 360 (a 360 is when subordinates, peers, or superiors rate a person on a number of job-related skills and behaviors) are overwhelmingly negative, the manager accepts the need for coaching. As is usually the case, before an executive can improve, he has to admit he has a problem. When our coaching efforts are not successful, it is often because the executive doesn't really think he should or has to change. Their true behavior is revealed in cancellations, investing little time or effort in the assignments, or being slow to return phone calls.

Another example of denial is when you credit yourself with "leadership" qualities and "high potential" when, in actuality, you're not in that league, according to your subordinates and peers.

So often when executives get fired, their response is, "I didn't see it coming." The signs you are falling out of favor are usually quite apparent, but oftentimes we deny that which is evident to others.

➜ Have you ever been "blindsided," but when you looked back all the signs were there?

Idealization

Overestimating an admired aspect or attribute of another is idealization. Businesspeople usually go through the life lesson of idealizing somebody only to discover that that person has deep faults they didn't want to recognize. Perhaps because they wanted something from the person, they idealized him. This is the "emperor's new clothes" syndrome. I once idealized a supervisor I had when I was interning to become licensed. Initially I thought the guy walked on water. Because I needed to do well on my internship, I believed only what I wanted to believe. Over time, however, I saw he was manipulative and deceitful. Although he was intelligent and well published, he lacked ethics and integrity.

→ Have you ever admired somebody, only to find out that he or she was not the person you thought?
→ How did this cause you to grow as a person?

Identification

Idealization often leads to identification. Identification is patterning oneself after someone else. When you exceed normal admiration and regard others' traits as your own, you block awareness of your own unique talents and abilities. On the other hand, appreciation of others' attractive attributes can indicate self-development possibilities.

→ Have you ever dressed or acted like somebody you admire? In the long run, did this actually cause your own growth to ebb?
→ Think about people you're attracted to and identified with. What qualities do they have?
→ How did you (or would you like to) change to become more like these people?

Rationalization

Justifying behavior or feelings is rationalization. For example, people who take advantage of others or who are unethical say to themselves, "He would have screwed me first if given the opportunity, so I had to screw him." I have known more than one executive intensely disliked by virtually their entire staff who rationalized the situation by saying to themselves, "Those people just don't realize the stress and obstacles I face. If they did, they would know how well I handle things." I have seen executives who have acted unethically, or at least dishonorably, yet defend their actions to themselves. You can imagine what these guys do for teamwork.

→ Think of a situation that made you feel shame. How did you rationalize that behavior to yourself when you actually did it?

Repression

Repression is another defense that we've all experienced. Repression means isolating your desires, impulses, wishes, fantasies, or feelings from your awareness by pushing them down into the unconscious. Repression comes into play to keep information and thoughts from entering your awareness. However, memories and thoughts don't vanish when repressed. Rather, they continue to affect behavior. For example, a person who had authoritarian parents may be an authoritarian boss and not be aware of it or how he got that way. Sometimes we "suppress" unwelcome thoughts. When we actively push insights out of awareness, we call this suppression. This is when we consciously force the unwanted information out of our awareness.

FREE ASSOCIATION

Let's try a technique that can be interesting and insightful. Close your eyes. Get relaxed. Look at your watch. Now, write down every word you can think of that pops into your mind. Don't monitor or restrict your words to be politically correct to yourself. Just let words flow into your awareness for one minute while you jot them down.

What you just did was a version of Sigmund Freud's technique of "free association." Freud developed this procedure as a means of access to the unconscious. He got his patients to relax and then asked them to say whatever words jumped into their conscious awareness. When the patient freely associated, the suppression or self-censorship of thoughts and feelings was eliminated. The patient did not edit what he said. Whatever was uppermost in the patient's mind poured forth. This allowed the patient to know himself more fully by understanding what the dominant theme of his mind was. At different points in the day, one has different themes, but over time, when done at multiple intervals, patterns emerge.

Freud encouraged patients to freely share thoughts. It makes no difference whether the words are logical, consistent, or socially appropriate. Even thoughts that seem inconsequential, strange, or uncomfortable should be verbalized without hesitation. Initially, free association is difficult. Most people, especially high-level executives who are used to being listened to very carefully, edit their thoughts. Westerners especially want to present ideas in a logical, linear way. People omit embarrassing words. They want to seem socially acceptable and "normal." But with practice and encouragement, patients learn that it's all right to be open and uninterrupted.

We can do the same thing here. As I've said before, it's only you and the book. There's no reason not to be totally honest. After all, you are your own business coach. The more closely you write down your stream of conscious, the more likely you are to gain insight into the real issues facing your life. Besides the subject matter of the words themselves, the connections between words offer important insights.

Free association is a free-flowing, intuitive technique. Neither therapist nor patient plans in advance or tries to direct where the rapidly expressed thoughts lead. But since the words and ideas spring from the patient's unconscious, the patient finds it enormously interesting and sometimes quite enlightening. The material that is brought forth matters very much to the patient even though she might not initially be aware of its meaning. There are no rules. Your goal is to allow your thoughts to flow freely. Sometimes you can run out of words because you are resisting.

Now, let's analyze what you've just written. In understanding associations between the words, the range of interpretations is vast. First off, there is a necessary cognitive shift you must make. In the above exercise, your mind was passive. You accepted whatever word popped into your head. But now we must change our approach to one of being active. Try to see the underlying association between your words—don't just look at a catalog of words that appear random.

The fact is, according to the basics of psychoanalysis, the words will usually have an underlying theme. Your job is to figure out, at least for this one minute of activity, what the theme is. Your goal is emotional insight. Go after what causes your curiosity. What seems to be the emotional truth in your string of words? What do you think the underlying theme that your unconscious was trying to express is?

It is here that we must trust our intuition. There is no other thing to trust. You will identify the theme when you are ready to accept it. In other words, we all have resistances when it comes to self-discovery. But by using the free association technique on yourself, you gain some insight into your underlying motivations. You will accept whatever you come up with.

Doing this several times over a period of weeks will show you that with each attempt you will come up with one connection at a time. Write about anything that comes to mind, whether it's important or inconsequential, meaningful or confused. You get the idea—whatever comes to you. As you allow yourself to relax,

your words will flow, but usually following a pattern that is deci-
pherable by you with some analysis.

> → What is your connection or observation or insight as to the
>   underlying theme of your word association?
> → How does this piece of information play itself out in your
>   life; that is, how does the theme manifest?
> → What are the consequences of the theme in your life?

As an example, here is what a young (twenty-eight–year-old)
MBA student recently wrote when I asked her to do this exercise:

Email
Table
Ants
Pen
Chair
Door
Book
Magazine
Paper
Weather
Window
Excel
Article

Note that the words were all things that were observable in her
surroundings (she had one of those plastic ant farms on her desk so
the word *Ant* isn't an anomaly!). What is the interpretation here?
She is more fixated on the visual here and now. Her life is all about
serving her internship with a venture capital fund, doing great work
in the present for the partner team. She reflected, when questioned,
that she is a visual person and enjoys being able to see something
more than to hear something. The point is that her unconscious is
saying that it wants to stay with the present, that getting things
done today is critical. Focus, focus . . . get that degree!
   Here is what a thirty-five-year-old, fast-paced, vigorous executive wrote:

Schedule
Energy
Economics
Sunny Day
Innovation
Selling

Friday
WSJ
Gift
Travel
IPO
Coffee

Let's examine the underlying theme. Here is a man committed to achievement. Note how the words *Schedule, Energy, Economics, Innovation, Selling, WSJ,* and *IPO* all tie together to provide a picture of his masculine unconscious that promotes originality in developing commercially successful business models. Note also some underlying desire to get away and relax from the stress of his day-to-day existence: *Sunny Day, Friday, Gift, Travel, Coffee.*

"HERE WE GROW AGAIN"

As the old saying goes, the only difference between a rut and a grave is the depth of the hole. It can take a person quite a while to become aware he isn't moving forward and is merely repeating behaviors. When things go pretty well, we have a tendency to replicate the same actions. Comfort zones are nice. But they need to be temporary if you're going to be successful in the long term.

Most people have adequate but modest confidence. Thus, we want to stay in an unpretentious comfort zone of least travails and resistance. Comfort and a trouble-free life are wonderful, in concept. But in reality we are here to work. Nobody has a comfortable or trouble-free life. Nor would you want it if you could have it. That sounds ridiculous, but when you understand that life at its core is an experiment, you become open to risks. It is the challenges that make life so worthwhile.

Our work could be business, parenting, philanthropy, or a support role, but we are all here to work. Seeking safety and predictability can subtly turn into a zone of mediocrity that diminishes potential. Your comfort zone can be your zone of weakness and laziness. The problem isn't so much a lack of challenge and growth opportunities as it is our lack of motivation. We get into a groove and tend to stay there. If you're going to hit the big time, you have to keep moving. It's a constant battle to take your business or career to the next level. Living life in safety is ultimately not what you were meant to do. Human beings have an innate desire to learn and grow. This need can be repressed due to our wanting safety.

→ When have you chosen safety over risk taking?
→ How did life ultimately put the same issue in front of you again and force you to grow?

It is nice to have periods in life where everything is firing on all cylinders. And we do have times like these. Enjoy them for what they are. But, when you get into a groove, it can slowly turn into an appeasing approach to life, which is the beginning of inevitable decline. Many of us work just hard enough not to get fired. We don't arrive fifteen minutes early and leave fifteen minutes after the boss.

In 2009, our country was facing tremendous financial pressure due to the subprime mortgage mess. Many people who were fat, dumb, and happy suddenly had the rug pulled out from under them. And, there were many hardworking, honest employees who got a pink slip for all their loyalty and caring. It seemed almost everybody was experiencing an undercurrent of anxiety. If ever there was a time to begin to think about one's career, future, and security, this was it.

"Security" is having the desire and inner confidence to become entrepreneurial and independent. It's blooming again across America.

If you are deeply opinionated and hold your opinions as fact, you don't engage in any type of intellectual discourse in your own mind. Be careful your deep-seated beliefs aren't holding you back or causing narrow-mindedness.

There is a small group of people who intuitively know there is something bigger and better for them out there. They go for it, never looking back or regretting their decisions. They move on with their lives. They conquer new territory even though they were comfortable and happy where they were. You've probably seen this characteristic in owners of thriving businesses or in some CEOs. Even though they are happy and successful, they lace up their shoes every Monday morning ready for battle. I know multimillionaires who easily could retire and play golf all day. Yet they work harder than anybody. They constantly strive to move their life to the next level.

OVERCOMING FEAR OF DREAMING TO BE GREAT

Anxiety signifies an inner doubt, and inner doubt metaphorically ties one hand behind your back. When you doubt, you don't think big—you only think of survival. And when you only think of survival, that's the level your career manifests. Fear is the great illusion. It holds us to a level below what we're capable of. If you're under anxiety and tension, it's difficult to be creative and open to insight and intuition.

Realize one thing—you're never, ever going to think of everything. It's impossible to visualize the entire spectrum of positives and negatives of any complicated decision. The unforeseen and unexpected can never be ruled out. You perceive only that which you are aware of. How about what you're not aware of? All you can do is to have confidence that you will be able to handle what's going to be thrown at you. This is the best mental preparation. Don't try to think of everything that could go wrong. Be mentally prepared through your belief in your ability to handle it.

One of the great discoveries is acknowledging you'll always have problems. Challenging yourself to creatively solve problems is playing the game of life at the expert level. When you overcome resentment of life's difficulties, you view problems as opportunities.

We've all heard statements and philosophies like this. On a deeper level we tend to dismiss them. We don't want problems. We don't want to see problems as an avenue for personal development.

Have confidence you are trying your best to be objective, and go do it. Be in the dark about some things. That's OK. We all are. We are going to turn up the lights on some key issues. If *Becoming Your Own Business Coach* does that for you, then that's great . . . call it a successful experience.

BECOMING AWARE OF BLOCKAGES

An important but difficult-to-recognize challenge for any attempt at executive growth is to want self-development, not self-aggrandizement. Too often in our consulting we observe participants who love self-growth. But they don't understand the underlying motivation for their zeal. Loving executive development is positive. Ask *why* you like it. How does the effort pay off for you?

The New Age movement from the late 1960s to the present spawned a cottage industry of phony growth: If you are feeling negative, grab a quartz crystal, meditate, and go into a trance. Those responses—while having some legitimacy, depending on one's perspective—do not address a deeper analysis of "self."

→ Think about an area of your life that is currently giving you psychic pain. Ask yourself, "What actions and behaviors have I taken to draw this energy to me?"

"Feeling better" is a worthwhile goal. But so is feeling responsibility. Learn insight from self-analysis. To change to a positive sustainable consciousness, psychological pain needs to be viewed as an honest friend. This pain tells you to become your own coach. Figure out how your behavior contributed to your negativity. Don't just try to be happy and move quickly past your discomfort.

In business, as most executives will attest, a recession is an excellent time to discover what your business needs to run effectively, what your competencies are, and whose company is built on a solid foundation instead of advertising and marketing hype. Think about depression, anxiety, and sadness as your recession.

Be optimistic about yourself and your chances for winning. Do you fundamentally see yourself as a good and worthy person who deserves success? Or, at some level, do you see yourself as someone who is destined to struggle and ultimately be mediocre?

You change to the degree that you are willing to change. There is always a self-protection or defense against information that is too threatening when that information is received. If you are given performance feedback, even if the critique has aspects of truth, you might reject it entirely if you aren't ready to change or to get critiqued.

Let's say you were called upon to give a presentation to your board of directors. You sweated bullets, worked hard on the PowerPoint, practiced in front of the mirror, and did relaxation exercises that morning, and it all went fine. It was all you could do to get up there and give the speech—but you did it, you made it happen. If afterwards somebody says, "Could I give you some feedback?" You might say, "Sure," but inside you are saying, "Screw you." Why? You needed to decompress after the board meeting. You needed to reflect upon your efforts, to turn the meeting over in your mind. Then, and only then, are you truly open to receiving other views.

"C Suite" executives are too often no smarter or better leaders than many people under them. Organizational manipulation, luck, or nepotism are the reasons they ended up where they are. However, if there are specific reasons that block you, then it is best those reasons be discovered and altered.

Perhaps you turn people off because of abrasiveness. Yet you condone that quality. You see the attribute as wanting to get at truth. But the real reason is hidden behind self-serving explanation. You won't ever progress until you come to grips with the real reason for your argumentativeness: a constant need to win.

If you have a high need for affection, you will attempt to receive it from all colleagues, at times inappropriately. If you have a high need for order, not only will your desk be spotless, but you will spend an inordinate amount of time hyper-collecting information instead of acting on it. If you have an independent streak, you might have a hard time reporting to anybody. You'll continually get fired regardless of the important skills you bring to the table.

Oftentimes what is painfully obvious to others is invisible to us. One way to better understand yourself is to reflect on what makes you anxious. Do you overly berate yourself when you make a mistake? The reason for this could be your perfectionism. If you can't stand authority, do you get into conflict with your supervisors?

→ What is it that makes you anxious?

You know from your own life experiences that the recognition of the areas you want to improve doesn't mean you *will* improve. Most readers will acknowledge they have habits and areas of their lives they would, ideally, like to change. But they are unwilling to put forth the effort. Or, the enjoyment or satisfaction from the behavior is such that it's not worth changing. Any smoker will openly tell you they would like to quit. But there is a certain psychological and physical pleasure from the act of lighting up that compels them to do it.

There is usually a liberating feeling when a person increases her insight into herself. But as we discover about ourselves, we want to change, yet we don't.

→ What behavior or habit of yours would you like to change, but the pleasure you derive from it is greater than your will to change?
→ Does your inability to gain enough motivation remind you that you're only too human?

A former client was a good example of someone who compulsively wanted to appear perfect. But he didn't want to change this outlook. There was no possibility of genuine development. Real change was out of his awareness. His only concern was to create a biography with no imperfections to preserve the covert feeling of superiority over others.

Many executives desire social prestige and power. Any acknowledged weakness to them is threatening, and they spend much time in convincing themselves and others of their distinction. They can sometimes be surprisingly successful in certain environments that favor style over substance.

The issues you have in life are determined by the image you have of yourself. Underperformers have poor truthfulness in self-evaluation. In performance reviews, they continually score themselves significantly higher on measures than their colleagues or bosses do.

Some executives have ability in quantitative measurement. CFOs in particular are, in virtually all cases, superior with numbers. The issue is that they overrate what can be accomplished by spreadsheets. They take an inflated pride in their power of judgment based on "the numbers." Too often have we seen CFOs, feeling smugly superior, belittling the sales team for their lack of numerical ability.

The same phenomenon can be observed in sales-oriented executives. They justify much behavior because of "gut instinct" and "intuition." Too often they dismiss logic. In both cases, it is pride of ego that stifles further development.

Executives who neurotically desire power and prestige judge others solely on how much of these qualities they have. The higher they move within an organization, the more they look down on those they have passed. If you have too high a need for affection, you will be self-righteously confident in your teamwork and be overly quick to point out how others are not team players.

→ How do you overly estimate the impact of your strengths?

For many people, prestige and standing are important parts of self-identity. And much leadership training involves the lowering of defense mechanisms. A good deal of role-playing occurs in training classes. The executive who needs stature doesn't want to appear awkward, so he cleverly finds ways of not attending. Or he takes a superficial face-saving approach to the experience. There is little spontaneity, and his responses are trite.

Some of us have considerable interest in asserting that things are better than they are. This is true in regard to sales. Often, salespeople have an overoptimistic view of their pipeline.

In general, the more unhealthy a person, the less he or she tolerates criticism. The less people want to change, the stronger and more impenetrable are their defense mechanisms.

One challenge of coaching yourself is time. If you have an appointment with your coach, you want to keep the appointment. There is a certain pressure to do so and social embarrassment if you miss. There is opportunity cost, a fee to be paid regardless of whether you used the hour or not, so it doesn't make sense to pay and not get the benefit.

But when you want to take a good look at yourself, there is no time set aside for doing so. How many of us set aside an hour a week for self-reflection or introspection? I would dare to suggest not many. But yet again another advantage in becoming your own business coach is that you can look at yourself anytime. When you feel an urge to engage in self-examination, it is always there for you.

All of us want to improve. Who wouldn't want to get rid of handicaps that are holding them back? All of us are for positive change. We want to get rid of the bad aspects of our personalities. But we want to keep aspects of our personalities that have proved to be of value or pleasure. We don't want to give up power, even when we realize our need for power is based on, for example, our desire to overcome an authoritarian father.

Getting to the root of this and identifying the source of your blockages is productive. But most executives, even when they realize the source of their ambition isn't as healthy as they once believed, don't want to relinquish power. Maybe an entrepreneur through coaching realizes a driver of his need for independence is his refusal to be bound by rules. Even though there is a renegade within that he doesn't allow his employees to have, he excuses himself.

The source of your internal resistance is your desire to maintain the status quo.

7

Becoming Confident

Let's get more self-confident right now! Give yourself credit. You are a hardworking, successful person. Sure, you have some issues and personal demons—so what? All things considered, you are leading a productive life. Give yourself a pat on the back every now and then. (God knows, nobody else will!)

→ How often do you reward or praise yourself when you have done well?
→ When was the last time?

Self-confidence is not a pervasive attribute. Typically, you'll enjoy areas of high and low confidence. We're all confident in specific arenas. For example, sales executives excel at selling, fostering interpersonal relationships, seeing opportunities, and public speaking. Perhaps, at the same time, these same highly confident people may lack faith in their ability to learn higher-order math, fix cars, or lay down processes to get organized. You might be confident selling, but when it comes to sitting down and learning a new computer program, your hands get clammy and the heart rate jumps.

Some people have natural rhythm and athletic ability. Some people know and trust intuition because it has served them well over the years. Others want hard-core, objective facts to guide them. So "self-confidence" isn't all encompassing. It depends on which facet of life is under consideration.

Yet when we talk of "being self-confident," we mean having an overarching, fundamental belief in one's competency to handle life. This is our primary goal in self-belief. Confidence means you know you tap into a core of strong positive feelings about yourself when faced with adversity, ambiguity, or both. You know you won't wither. You'll make it to the other side of the river of life. You know you possess talents worthy of respect, both from yourself and others.

> *The story of the human race is the story of men and women selling themselves short.*
>
> —Abraham Maslow

Good executives understand that there are areas they feel unsure of. They believe they can acquire those skills or, more likely, find somebody they trust to partner with to handle the work or build those competencies. They feel certain they will discover solutions or find someone who can help.

If you lack this basic "I can" attitude, the chances of making it to the C suite dissipate pretty aggressively. Unless you have this core set of beliefs, you won't have the courage to take full responsibility of leadership. Your attitude toward achieving your goal is as important as your skill set in reaching the goal.

> *Attitudes are more important than facts.*
>
> —Karl Menninger

SOURCES OF SELF-CONFIDENCE

No single factor is responsible for the development of self-confidence. Parents' behavior and attitudes are fundamental to children's feelings and self-perception. This is particularly true in childhood. When Mom or Dad or some other loving significant adult figure is accepting and encouraging and allows a child the dignity of asking questions and getting genuine responses, the child begins the foundation of positive self-regard. This is even more true when a mother is supportive of her son or a father supportive of his daughter.

In contrast, if parents or other significant adults are overly critical, strict, emotionally rigid, or belittling, children may soon believe they are incapable or inferior. When you were growing up, possibly your parents didn't provide you with an environment that said, "Go for it." As a result, you subconsciously don't believe you can become a successful top-level executive or entrepreneur. Confidence-eroding incidents can be buried in a person's psyche outside awareness. When faced with adversity, he withers, or when faced with ambiguity, she freezes. Through the processes being advocated throughout this book, we need to gain awareness of several factors that could hold us back from achieving our vision.

Life shrinks or expands in proportion to one's courage.
—Anaïs Nin

When parents encourage moves toward self-reliance and accept when mistakes are made, children accept themselves. When these children grow up and make mistakes in their careers (like everyone does), they don't get depressed and throw in the towel. They reflect, analyze, learn, and move on.

→ Were you more criticized or supported when growing up?
→ How do you think early life criticisms still affect you?
→ Did the way you were raised help, hurt, or have no discernable effect on your confidence in believing you can become a top executive or entrepreneur?

Resolve to yourself right now to forgive and forget any unsupportive parenting issues and move forward!

Surprisingly, people can have all the ability in the world, yet lack self-confidence because of some perceived lack of accomplishment earlier in their life. I have seen this with highly successful entrepreneurs who achieved great things but secretly doubted themselves because they had dropped out of college. We work with people of enormous talent who confide to us of their inner sadness and doubt. Even though they are successful, their doubt hinders them from unfolding their highest potential, or at least enjoying their lives more. You have seen people who are successful by virtually any standard, but never seem to truly enjoy success. Self-confidence can help lead to success, but there are many successful people without self-confidence. Still, the attribute is wonderful to have. It makes life more fun and enjoyable. And isn't that what it is all about?

We all have traits, abilities, and skills that are above average. Instead of allowing these to mold our self-confidence, though, we tend to focus on unrealistic expectations, others' standards, or our weak areas. If I based my self-esteem on how I compare to a great behavioral scientist such as Carl Jung, I would feel I was a total loser! Instead, I base my self-esteem on contributing to the success of others, enjoying quality relationships, being at inner peace, and having a profession I am good at and that I enjoy. There are downers and disappointing days, but these only serve to make success much sweeter.

→ We all experience lack of confidence at some point or in some areas. What are you not confident about?

→ Is this a specific ability (e.g., you can't do calculus) or an encompassing mindset?

EXECUTIVE CONFIDENCE SCALE

In the quiz below, circle the letter that best describes how you feel.

1. When confronted by a series of critical circumstances when you need to make a series of "rapid-fire" decisions, you become anxious.
   a. No
   b. Occasionally
   c. Yes

2. You solidly believe you have some excellent talents, abilities, and skills.
   a. Yes
   b. Uncertain
   c. No

3. I share my advice with my clients and/or coworkers about ways I think they can improve their business or productivity regardless of whether they ask my viewpoint.
   a. Yes
   b. Sometimes
   c. No

4. When I reflect on my behavior, I think I take calculated risks.
   a. Yes
   b. Sometimes
   c. No

5. When a work study committee is formed and I think I am the most qualified to lead it, I step up to the leadership role and control the team dynamics.
   a. Yes
   b. Not often
   c. No

6. I enjoy being "behind the microphone" in most situations.
   a. Yes
   b. Occasionally
   c. No

7. Other executives are more gifted than me.
   a. No
   b. Sometimes
   c. Yes

8. Most of the time I'm the leader in my work team even though we're all technically peers.
   a. Yes
   b. Sometimes
   c. No

9. I like to take control and make things happen; I love being given responsibility.
   a. Yes
   b. Not often
   c. No

10. Speaking in front of a large meeting of customers at a trade show would make me nervous.
    a. No
    b. To some extent
    c. Yes

11. I describe myself as resilient and bold.
    a. Yes
    b. Occasionally
    c. No

Count each (a) as one, each (b) as two, and each (c) as three. How high was your score?

Count each (a) answer as two points, each (b) as one point, and each (c) as zero points. Add your scores to find your total. The higher the score, the more interpersonally confident you tend to be:

- 18–22: Strong level of leadership self-confidence
- 11–17: Above-average level of leadership self-confidence
- 6–10: Moderately low level of leadership self-confidence
- 0–5: Low level of leadership self-confidence

YOUR PROBLEMS

→ Reflecting on life, are there objective, hard facts you think support the idea that you've had more than your fair share of failures or hardships? What's the evidence?

We ask the question above because most of us get consumed with our own problems and think that, for some reason, there are extra burdens on us. You're *supposed* to face trials and tribulations. That's the way life is. Your problems are no more or less than those faced by the vast majority of people who surround you. Obviously, people who exist on a dollar a day in squalid conditions have many different problems, but this doesn't mean they can't be happy. A person can be poor, but if they are grateful for what they have, don't envy others, and find happiness in simplicity, they can be very happy regardless of conditions. When life is a constant struggle, one does not stop to ponder happiness, acquire self-insight, or reflect on the inner self. When people are consumed by survival instincts, they spend much of their lives in the unconscious state where they try to gather the simple resources to live another day.

The fact that you're challenging yourself to grow implies you're in the minority of people who have the guts and the wherewithal to try to improve. Feel lucky and grateful you have this mindset. It takes a certain confidence and seriousness to challenge yourself to improve. But once you've made a commitment, it tends to be an enjoyable state. Setting goals, reaching them, and then stretching again is a splendid way to live.

KEEP FRUSTRATION IN PERSPECTIVE

Frustration, over time, leads to anger. When we get angry, we lose control and we then do dumb things. When you're frustrated by obstacles or challenges, react appropriately. Keep it in perspective. This is hard to do. Ever notice how differently things look in the morning? When you get a piece of disappointing news (and the fact is we get quite a bit of this type of information), consider the obstacle for what it is—then try to remove it. Most events have an upside to them if you look hard enough. Some don't. Ultimately you have to accept the fact you got screwed, that you got beaten in a lousy deal, that people weren't loyal . . . whatever—and move on.

> → When is the last time you decided to "sleep on it" and came to a different conclusion because of it?

When have you gotten screwed? Have you gotten over it? Or does it still bother you? Resolve now to let it go! And be thankful for the valuable life lesson. Say out loud now: "I forgive my adversary. May my life continue in peace. I release all anger."

Try to not overgeneralize. People overgeneralize when they say things like, "I'm having a bad day." Sure, you might have had things go wrong, but don't overgeneralize and label the whole day as "bad." Believe that whatever was causing the frustration is temporary. You can solve it. I'm not suggesting that if something really bad happens, you can't go to pieces. That's natural and appropriate. But when you allow unconnected events to become connected and then aggregate them into a massive frustration, you've set yourself up for negativity and a lack of productivity. The problem is solitary, an event and only an event or set of circumstances. We can get so focused on our frustrations and difficulties that we forget our original vision. People want to do business with positive people. Don't you?

→ What are your biggest frustrations?
→ How confident are you that you'll overcome them?
→ Are there some situations you encounter that trigger your emotions?
→ Now, when you reflect on the above question, do you think you have overreacted?

You're going to have victories and defeats. Remember your victories when you're depressed! Take time and savor the occasional successes. Appreciate what you've created. Look forward to dreaming up new, exciting pathways to success after you've arrived at your destination.

Don't think about the future *so* much that your mind constantly lives there. The present is more important than the future. It's the past you forget. Take only the hard-won lessons of success and failure. One of the things I have learned is to be present oriented. In my youth, I was so focused on the future that too often I didn't appreciate the present—the only place where we actually live our lives.

When you fail to overcome a difficult challenge and quit, that particular type of challenge grows stronger. We usually end up facing the problem again in another form, and it's much harder to overcome when we backed down the first time. Like the proverbial bully harassing you in third grade, the more you try to run, the harder it gets to challenge the problem. Draw the line and fight it out, even if you get beat up. The bullying stops when you confront the challenge head-on.

→ When in life have you given up too quickly?
→ Do you have issues in your life now you are backing down from?

KEEP EVENTS IN PROPORTION

Great accomplishments are the result of a steady march forward with emotional self-discipline. Don't you know people (maybe you're one of them) who manipulate their lives into a psycho-drama? Every day there is a new crisis, new people out to get them, a new calamity the universe dumps on them.

For some people, letting their emotions run wild is fun. It gives a sense of power to have adrenaline run through their system. They feel empowered and dominant temporarily. The feeling is an illusion, created only to thwart anxiety through temporary feelings of control. They may believe they can manipulate their environment by their emotionality (and sometimes they can). People around them become enablers. It's not healthy. It diminishes effectiveness as the leader. It leads to a loss of respect. It sends the message they're not in control; their emotions are. If a leader sends this message frequently, his days as a leader are numbered.

SEE REALITY

View events in their true state of reality. For example, opportunities at the outset of a new venture or idea may look promising, but the venture can fail miserably if we lack the ability to see all the obstacles. We may miscalculate and underestimate problems. Conversely, seemingly hopeless situations can sometimes turn out to be great opportunities. When things look hopeless, we see all the ways it can't work. Winners look at the whole situation realistically but creatively.

When you are running a business and you've tried a number of different approaches and offerings but customers aren't buying, you realize that if you're going to stay in business, you're going to have to offer a whole new approach. In a commodity-driven market especially, how do you differentiate yourself?

Other competitors and other people aren't the enemy; your emotional reaction is the enemy. Stopping emotional reaction is, for some people, much of the battle. When you're calm and collected, you think, reason, and visualize better.

So many things that initially look lousy turn out to be blessings in disguise. You take on a new job only to discover how different your values are from the company you joined, and you have to leave after a year. At first you might be disappointed. But think to yourself, "I'm totally responsible for what happens in my life. My decision could work to my advantage. I can create my own future." And you will—with far greater rewards than you ever could have had by staying with a company you were a bad fit for.

Every day, we face tough situations. We make tough decisions running our business, division, or work group. The more you emotionally react, the greater the likelihood of failure. Yes, you can show me how people who are highly emotional lead successful companies. However, we are talking about the long run here. People who are emotionally reactive, even if they get off to a good start, tend to crater in the long term. If you can resist immediate gratification, not reacting to events but embracing them, you'll lay the groundwork for success. It's much better than blowing up every few hours.

All day long, you have decisions to make about how you're going to react to rejection, uncertainty, disappointment, and so on. Don't get down on yourself. You may get angry or disappointed with yourself, because you're only human and can't help but occasionally be down, discouraged, and irate. You may feel resentful toward customers for not understanding how your ideas can help them, or toward the aloof secretary when you cold-call or the indifferent coworker. But the more you choose the proactive, positive alternative, the more certain and confident you become.

NO MORE EXCUSES!

Successful executives, over the long term, eventually arrive at a fundamental orientation. This attitude is a mental building block from which there is no substitution or equivocation: *Take full responsibility for everything that happens.* Accept the fact that the ball is hit into your court virtually every day.

This orientation is harder than it initially appears. Some corporate executives are quite skilled at ingeniously blaming other people when things don't go well. (This is termed "organizational savvy" in the literature.) They're equally accomplished at inserting themselves in the limelight when things go well. But when you are a field executive and have total control over profit and loss, there's nowhere to run or hide; there's nobody else to blame. This is intimidating. The power and freedom you seek carry with them a price most people *say* they want, but really don't: responsibility—total and complete personal accountability.

As is usually the case, a total-responsibility orientation is easier to write about than to actualize. How many of us say, "She made me mad," or blame others when things don't go our way? We do it more often than we care to admit. For example, virtually every time you get frustrated or angry, the emotional part of you wants to blame somebody or something. It's a natural defense mechanism. When you reflect on your emotions, however, you arrive at the realization that you *allowed* people to make you angry.

The fact is you did have a choice. Resolve to yourself you're going to develop the mental toughness, and the life philosophy, that you—and only you—will take responsibility for your success or failure. It's not the market's fault. Nor the fault of customers who don't take or return phone calls. It is the concept of total responsibility that scares away managers from wanting to dream big and be responsible for profit and loss. When you're inside a company and things go wrong, there is usually somebody else to blame. One corporate president whom I admire puts it like this: "Everybody stands up and points to the guy on his left."

You have the ability to turn desire into reality, but you must take responsibility. Be willing to put in the work. When things go south, people usually don't suggest it's due to something personal (effort, ability) but instead ascribe blame to external problems beyond their control—obstacles, constraints, inadequate resources or support, different departments or divisions withholding information, market conditions . . . whatever.

Positive, upbeat people energize those around them. Their energy is infectious. Upbeat people avoid ruminating about problems and events. While not blaming themselves, they're able to take responsibility. The critical differentiation: responsibility versus blame. The minute you blame other people, bad luck, timing, or life not being fair, you lose the essence of psychological strength, which is taking responsibility for your thoughts, attitudes, and actions. Blaming leaves you busy finding fault that causes the negative emotion of guilt. Responsibility is accountability minus the emotional overtones.

MOTIVATING YOURSELF—IT'S YOUR SHOW!

Motivation isn't due solely to ability. There's a correlation between ability and motivation. The intervening variable is confidence. The more confidence you have you'll succeed, the harder you'll work. If you believe, you'll put forth effort. When somebody senses that if they work hard they'll attain goals, they will work harder than other people who don't believe they can be successful. Bright people are confident because they know they're bright. They can do certain things not everybody can do. This confidence helps them accumulate a successful track record. When they get ready to take a plunge, they have mental stamina.

We can't *see* motivation, only behavior. As an employer, you can administer environmental stress. For example, the threat of punishment causes "motivation" in order to escape punishment. In the corporate world, fear of punishment is a prime motivator. But fear isn't intrinsic; it's extrinsic motivation—a force from outside the person which is impacting that person's behavior. A senior executive needs to be internally motivated. For the most part, there is no calling in sick, no designated coffee breaks at ten. There's no overtime, quotas, or recognition awards. It's all up to her, every day.

The ability to challenge yourself, innate curiosity, a feeling of control, and fantasizing about success—all are within you. Competition, cooperation, and recognition are motivators that stem from other persons; they are extrinsic. Executives must be motivated by the intrinsic and allocate for the extrinsic when it is available. The higher you go, the more you need to recognize yourself. There's nobody else. High levels of effort are associated with high levels of success.

One of the rewards of being a successful leader is gaining more control over your life. The energizing force that causes you to get up early and take aggressive action all day every day appears to stem from a type of internal tension; there's an inner drive that must be satiated. Business becomes more important than relaxation or a laidback, more balanced lifestyle. You choose to initiate effort, expend energy, and persist in the face of adversity. The motivation stems from your own psyche.

What you do every day (staying on task) and how hard and how long you work are all internally driven; there's no external regulation. Only your career and the marketplace guide you. You become addicted to the everyday effort. And often that addiction is positive and energizing. Work–life balance is important. *But when you truly are positively energized by what you do and how you do it, balance is not necessary.* Executives often don't lead a "well-balanced" life. There are restrictions placed on other interests. Staying in good physical shape, spiritual alignment, maintaining focus on the family and supportive friends, and little else forms a winning career.

> *Ideas not coupled with action never become bigger than the brain cells they occupied.*
> —Arnold H. Glasow

A form of intrinsic motivation more prominent than commonly appreciated is seeking business and social prominence in your city. You want to "be somebody"—a woman about town, someone recognized for her outstanding achievements, one people think highly of and want to know. You want to be one of the city's leading businesspeople, to have access to power and the right circle of acquaintances, and to have the ear of decision makers. Make no mistake—this is a strong drive for many.

It's not all bad to have a need for admiration. What's wrong with wanting to be a big shot and have money, power, and fame in your hometown? Nothing at all. It helps to imagine yourself in this role. Visualize how you'll look and act when you've made it. Don't let your ego take over or fantasize without putting in the effort. But there's nothing wrong with wanting to prove yourself and be recognized.

An idea is one thing. The process that leads the idea into manifestation is entirely different. Just because you have a good idea and are willing to work hard, that isn't a guarantee of success. Good ideas and hard work are the minimum, not the maximum, requirement. Be focused and willing to bring the idea into physical reality. With timing and good luck, it will happen. There are always certain energies from the outside that have to come to pass before the potential is actualized. And until those situations are addressed, the idea remains dormant. But the longer we focus and the more restrictions we place on other pursuits, the faster will be the movement toward our goal.

Ideas come easily to most people. However, only a small percentage of us can focus and dedicate the time and energy necessary to bring the pieces together to form a successful major innovation, especially if the company is large. Without push and drive, ideas remain unrealized, locked in your mind. Make your vision concrete. The faster you bridge the gap between the reality of the present and your vision, the greater your motivation. *Speed is a good thing, because it represents your degree of motivation.*

BEING AUTHENTIC

Authenticity is congruency between words and actions—being genuine. This starts with being comfortable with you. Self-disclose and share appropriately. Poke a little fun at yourself. It can take a lifetime to feel comfortable with who you are as a person. The ability to occasionally laugh at yourself helps.

It is liberating when one acknowledges a weakness, or sees how a strength is used successfully. You no longer have a hidden quality to yourself. The "self" issue is out from under the barrel. It can be acknowledged and accepted for what it is. There is almost a feeling of relief, an "aha" that says, "Now that I recognize this quality, I can deal with it. Or just accept it without further ado."

If you consistently get feedback that says you are a poor listener, you then have a clear recognition of a problem that is holding you back. You now have definition to the problem. Listening is a learnable skill. You can mobilize your resources and motivation. The fact that you are open to performance feedback demonstrates you are strong enough and capable of remediation and improvement. By the solitary act of reading this book, you know that there is nobody to blame or attack. You can proceed, or not, according to your own wishes. There is no need to argue or defend, as in the case of much performance feedback.

It is always tempting to make others responsible for your own shortcomings. By completing this book's exercises, you make yourself responsible. It is inspiring to do independent work. To grow is to gain an inner strength and confidence. For example, I recently established a rapport with a would-be client. Then, like many others reading this can identify with, I got "blown off"; my phone calls and email went unreturned. Because of my quality work with other companies, opportunities are coming in the door faster than we can respond. Thus not only don't we need this client, but her "snub" is less personally threatening.

We are validated by other, more impressive people. This happens more acutely in sales, as those in sales can readily testify. How many times have you tried really hard to help a new client, only to be rejected through no fault of your own? Then, surprisingly, other more interesting and lucrative clients who value your efforts show up, almost magically. You rapidly forget the old possible client and are grateful that the sale didn't consummate.

One of the pleasures of aging is that you care less and less if people like you or not. There is a freedom from worry about that type of thing. Not that you don't try to exhibit good social skills and emotional intelligence. Of course you do. It's just that sometimes you don't care whether you're liked or not. If you have a certain set of values and an aggressive, opinioned person disagrees with you, do you care whether he likes you or not?

Our emotions, perceptions, and behaviors are shaped by our most dominant thoughts. What you say to yourself powerfully influences your success; the energy of your inner dialogue, both positive and negative, determines much of your life. Over time, our recurrent thoughts turn into motivations which we manifest positively and negatively. The more positive self-affirmations you give yourself, the more optimistic, confident, and resilient you become.

Remember, our behavior changes as we change our thinking. You have the power to control your behavior by controlling your internal thinking. Begin to become positive by monitoring and governing your "self-talk." All of your psyche has to be channeled toward your goals. Your words stay positive with the attitude of determination. Focus on the image in your mind's eye to becoming the person you know, deep in your heart, that you can and will be.

Thoughts precede feelings. Your goal is to control your feelings as much as possible, through thinking. It is thinking that should rule our emotional state and decision making. We recognize and appreciate how powerful emotions are; at times, they are significantly more powerful than reasoning or thinking.

Regardless of culture or society, the ability to control one's temperament is universally admired. Indeed, at the very foundation of emotional maturity lies the concept of emotional control. Unless you own the company, you can't be the CEO unless you can control your temper. This statement isn't totally true, but it is so nearly true as to be a given.

We all have times in our lives where we act irrationally because our feelings overwhelm our thinking. The more mature a person becomes, though, the less this happens to them. At the time of this writing, Barack Obama is president of the United States. One of the reasons he won the 2008 election is that people perceived him as being a grounded, rational, and confident person who is in control of his emotions. During the presidential debates, it was clear he had the ability to keep his emotions from getting in the way of his thinking and responding. This was an important element in his election victory.

Try to override the feeling level when it works against you. When faced with a decision, if you react emotionally, determine your motivation. What is the seed of the feeling? We have many thoughts, but it is our feelings and emotions that propel us to act.

→ Can you remember a time when your feelings overrode your thinking?
→ How did this work against you?
→ Reflecting back, how could you have done a better job in "thinking" your way through the issue instead of emotionally responding?

Through positive inner dialogue, you can reach for the stars and figure out a pathway there. But our challenge is that too much of our self-talk is negative. Maybe we're not even aware of it. When a child hears over and over she isn't good enough, she tends to believe it and act accordingly. Years later, the same tapes play over again on the unconscious level, sabotaging her success. In the reverse, when people begin to think of themselves as smart, they begin to achieve academically. They seek to confirm their self-impressions; their attainments become a self-fulfilling prophecy. Many studies confirm these phenomena.

I remember clearly one event in my own life. During college, I was a pretty good student, especially the last three semesters when I became more focused. But I never considered myself "smart." I managed to get into a first-rate graduate school because I am a fairly good salesperson and had a good entrance interview. This particular graduate school had an interesting curriculum. It was a long program, requiring seventy-two graduate hours to get completely through it. After the first year and a half, the graduate students had to take a series of comprehensive exams to assess how well they understood statistics, abnormal psychology, personality tests, human motivation, human growth and development, and other topics in counseling and school psychology. If you did not do well, you got the consolation prize of a master's degree, but you did not get into the second half of the program in which students became certified as psychologists. I had pretty much decided I was going to be part of the crowd who didn't make it. In fact, I had told my landlord I was moving at the end of the semester. (I didn't show a whole lot of confidence in myself, did I?) Another twist in the saga was that the names of the top five students, those who scored the highest on all the tests, were posted as a form of recognition. I studied hard, figuring I would give it my best shot. Why not? What did I have to lose?

When I arrived at my class the week after the exams, a friend came up to me and said, "Congratulations." I asked him why. He replied that I ranked number four of all the graduate students who took the exams and my name was on the "Top Five" list. I had to go look for myself, and yes, there I was. As I began to reflect on my achievement, I began to view myself differently and decided I was in the same league as people who went on for a doctoral degree. And that's what I did, getting my doctorate. I wasn't any smarter than I was before the exams. It was my self-perception that changed, and my behavior correspondingly changed. My point is that when we send ourselves new, positive, and affirming messages, our behavior begins to mirror those messages.

As I sit here typing, I am thinking to myself, "I will get this book finished; I will get it published." And, as you realize if you are reading this, it worked! Right now, make a positive affirmation about your career: I will . . .

Inner dialogues can be self-delusional, and thus you can act on faulty data. We discussed this earlier when we talked about how your introspection can be faulty. Affirmations need to be grounded and credible so that when you say them, they resonate within you as truth. Affirmations need to be predicated on the non-ego-infused perception of reality. Use clearness and truth to undo negative thinking that has undermined your confidence.

It does you no good to say, "I will be CEO of this company in a year's time," when you are middle management. But you can say that you are going to achieve more than is required, or that you are going to see a connection between two problems and make an original contribution and receive recognition. You can say you are going to increase your sales 30 percent regardless of the economy.

Affirmations are best when positively stated. To say you are going to be more self-disciplined and not be late for work isn't as strong as saying you are going to be the first to arrive at work three days a week. Use words like "It's my responsibility to make it happen" or "I want to achieve my goals." Negative thoughts are pushed back by positive affirmations. To do this, you can use self-endorsements to build confidence, and change negative behavior patterns into positive patterns.

> *The greatest discovery of my generation is that human beings can alter their lives by altering their attitudes of mind.*
> —William James

Thoughts are real things. They aren't simple or unimportant. Thoughts make or break us. Constant doubt, anxiety, and worry pull us down. "As we think, so we will be" is a powerful statement. Think positively and expansively, without letting your ego run wild. Then, it's only a matter of time before it is brought into physical reality.

Thought awareness is when you monitor your thoughts to become aware of your own judgments (which are too often negative) running through your head. You are usually not aware of the thoughts you repeat to yourself on a continuing basis. But when you choose to be aware, you can be. Remember this fact: thoughts create reality. When you berate yourself and call yourself stupid, you start believing it. Often when you challenge negative thoughts, they disappear because they're so obviously wrong. They persist because they escape notice by your consciousness.

When doing the simple exercise below, don't suppress any thoughts—just let them run their course while you observe them, like a second person observing you, with no emotion. In the stillness of your own mind, notice if any negatives pop up. Normally in the daily course of your life, these appear and disappear, barely being noticed.

CONFRONTING YOUR CRITIC

Say to yourself out loud: "I am going to be hugely successful!"

➔ For the next minute (quickly), write down your stream of consciousness while you keep repeating to yourself: "I am going to be hugely successful!"

Did you judge, criticize, or negatively react to the statement? Did you think about how great it would be if you did become hugely successful? Consider how these tendencies play on your self-confidence. Negativity slips into your subconscious day-in and day-out. Thought awareness is the ground floor of the skyscraper of eliminating negative thinking. You can't counter thoughts you don't fully acknowledge. Did any of the negative thoughts in the above exercise have any true basis in reality? Probably not!

> *They are able because they think they are able.*
>
> —Virgil

Use self-talk to counter harmful assumptions. Practice catching yourself making wrong leaps of logic or negative comments and assumptions. Tell yourself, "Stop!" Take out the old, tired assumptions and replace them with invigorated ones. For example, when you notice yourself doubting your ability or resources to become the person you were meant to be, remind yourself that even if this is not quite the right time, you're going to arrange your life to pursue your dream over the long haul. This means you can accept yourself while still striving to create. When you think there is no way you could ever be successful in rising to the top of the business pyramid, challenge the thought right then. Say to yourself, "What's the evidence I'm not good enough?" Self-confidence means being realistic and grounded, but employing creative thinking and holding the belief you have the ability to do it. Guess what? You do!

➔ How often do you evaluate the outcome of your actions more harshly than you deserve?

The curious paradox is that when I accept myself just as I am, then I can change.

—Carl Rogers

Let's say that a manager wants to become a more trusted advisor to his boss. He has ideas he thinks can help the organization. But he feels too intimidated, particularly in group situations, to share his view. After some time, he becomes discouraged. But finally he discovers that his lack of self-confidence is because he has a high need to be liked. He can't stand the thought his ideas might be rejected. Now he has an immediate change in his outlook and his mood. Nothing has changed in his environment. Yet, being armed with this new knowledge gives him hope. Now there is a possibility of goal-directed action. By knowing that he has a high need to be liked, he can go through the cognitive analysis to challenge his beliefs. He can say to himself, "Where is the proof that somebody has to be liked all the time?"

When you are truly happy, you look at life with the feeling of being thankful for what you have and what you have achieved. There is objectivity and stoicism. When you consistently achieve, you have the ability to continue to talk to yourself in a positive and upbeat way, whatever the world throws at you. Winners are even-keeled, centered, and rational, particularly when in leadership roles. One of the worst mistakes a leader can make is being emotionally uncontrollable. It diminishes confidence.

→ Think about the role you have in your company for a minute. What feelings are you just now experiencing?
→ Do you like how you feel about your role? If not, change things for the better.

SELF-ENDORSEMENTS

Think these self-endorsements to yourself (or if there is nobody around, say them out loud!). Don't worry about sounding corny. When you repeat "can do" messages to yourself, your brain begins to register these thoughts. If these don't apply, then make up a few similar ones that do.

- I can become a top-level senior executive and make things happen.
- I am going to open my own business!
- I can achieve my goals—I'm not giving up!
- I am who I am, and I'm proud of myself!

- I am completely in control of my life and my career and that's that.
- I make mistakes. So what? I've learned a lot about life that way, and that's what we're here to do.
- I'm proceeding along with my life beautifully, and it's unfolding the way it's supposed to.
- I am a good person. I do good things for others. I have people who love me.
- I will approach my life as a beautiful opportunity to learn and open myself to new possibilities.
- I don't need to receive love, recognition, approval, or accolades from all the people that are meaningful to me. I believe in my personal standards and values for my life.
- I'm inherently worthy. I don't have to be number one, the winner, or excellent in all I do.
- My past is my past. It doesn't control my feelings toward myself. I will choose what influence I will allow it to have on my life.
- I will evaluate myself independently. I won't buy into the negative opinions of others. My own opinion about me gives me a strong sense of self.
- I won't ever give my personal power of belief in myself to others.

→ Write a positive statement that counters the burden you've carried all your life, right here, right now!

SELF-DEFEATING THOUGHT PATTERNS

Buying into hypotheses or conjectures can leave you vulnerable to self-defeating patterns of thinking such as:

- *All-or-nothing thinking.* "I'm a total failure when my business career is off track." You're not a total failure. This attitude assures you won't be happy much of the time. This black-or-white thinking causes you a lot of anxiety, too. So stop it; your career is fine.
- *Seeing only the negative.* Disaster is everywhere and is expected. Even a passing comment made in jest, or an opinion shared that isn't in conformance to your reality, darkens the mood and day. "I didn't make one sale today. I'm going to starve and be a failure."
- *Exaggerating the worst outcome, or minimizing the positive outcome.* The glass isn't just half-empty—the glass is the only drinking container in the kitchen. "Yeah, I really helped that client, but they probably won't come back. That's the way my life goes—lousy."

- *Irrational acceptance of emotions as truth.* "I feel like I can't make it, and if I feel that way, I must be right."
- *Tyranny of the shoulds and musts.* "Should" and "must" statements are often absolutes rather than reflective of your true wants and desires. "I should have the courage to ask for a promotion; if I don't, it just proves I lack courage."
- *Labeling.* Labeling communicates guilt. "I'm a stupid loser, and I'd fail if I tried to do anything great anyway."
- *Difficulty accepting compliments.* "You liked my presentation? I thought I rambled and put half the audience to sleep."

Have you ever been driving and needed to concentrate on directions? Did you turn the radio down? Why do you do that? The radio was blocking the subarticulation of you talking to yourself. You intuitively know driving performance is impaired unless you have the quiet to concentrate. The radio interferes with your inner speech, and thus it is a distraction.

We think in language; we are linguistic by nature. Instead of talking out loud, when introspecting you think and talk within. But it is still a form of language. We talk to ourselves much like we talk to others. This point of view has its critics, but when I "thought" about it, I thought in English sentences, engaging in "inner speech." From this frame of reference, I want to encourage you in "talking" to yourself in clear and unambiguous speech. As I write these words, I am subvocalizing to myself before my hands work the keyboard. For me, and probably for you, too, inner discussions are verbal. When we hear our boss's words in our head, it is a verbal working memory.

When you talk to yourself, use adjectives to better understand how you feel about a situation. The better your "feeling" vocabulary, the more your insights are enhanced. For example, adjectives such as *angry, annoyed, anxious, ashamed, bewildered, combative, confused, defeated, defiant, depressed, disgusted, embarrassed, envious, foolish,* and *frightened* are all feeling words you can use to articulate to yourself how you feel. Instead of thinking, "I am really mad at Sarah for never calling me back," try going deeper and with more self-responsibility: "My feelings are hurt because I thought I meant more to Sarah; her never returning my call is confusing." As is always the case, the more personal responsibility you take for the events in your life, the more mature you will become.

Great, happy, fortunate, splendid, confident, elated, lucky, serene, strong, important, special—just put these into sentences and write down your feelings. This will produce quick results, guaranteed.

→ I feel great because . . .
→ I am happy because . . .
→ One of the reasons that I feel special is because . . .
→ I am fortunate in that . . .
→ I will achieve my goals because . . .

> *The happiness of your life depends upon the quality of your thoughts: therefore, guard accordingly, and take care that you entertain no notions unsuitable to virtue and reasonable nature.*
> —Marcus Aurelius

When you talk to yourself with depth and acknowledge how you feel, you become open and honest. And this is the whole point: becoming less self-delusional and seeing the world with greater objectivity. The goal is reducing mistakes based upon wishful thinking or only looking at facts which support your thinking.

We talk to ourselves, from simple declarations such as "I don't want to forget to put my house keys in my bag before I close the door" to deep conversations such as "I hope I develop into a better person by overcoming my addiction."

Psychologists have long recognized that it is not the *event* that determines how you respond internally, but how you *interpret* the event. Interpretation begins with self-talk. For example, as I write these words, the world is experiencing a financial meltdown with thousands of people getting laid off every day. Unemployment is expected to move beyond 10 percent, and those who are not getting laid off are worrying a lot more. Certainly job loss is stressful; stress tests have been around for thirty years and confirm these disruptive events often lead to physical problems. But when you become overly negative or fearful about being laid off, or feel shameful and continuously discouraged, it begins to form your opinion of yourself. As I write this, seemingly self-confident people are being examined for depression.

Positive self-talk means substituting "situation" for "problem." A problem is a difficulty, trouble, or struggle that represents a potential loss. Situations are questions or puzzles that need solving. It's the same event, but how you interpret it changes how you feel. As a situation, it is different because you have more positive emotions to handle and solve the issue.

What is a "problem" in your life that, by substituting the word "situation," you will immediately feel better about? For example,

"My problem is I was laid off" becomes "My situation is I am seeking a new fulfilling opportunity."

OK, how about substituting the word "challenge" for "problem"? When you are faced with a possible layoff, instead of saying, "I am going to get the ax," say, "I am going to be facing an interesting and challenging set of dynamics in my career." This is such a more positive way of approaching the event. You now feel that getting laid off is something you rise to and that will make you stronger. Again the word you use to describe something makes it different. Now you believe that you are more powerful, can rise to this challenge, and will come out ahead of the game. Your response is different because you have repositioned the event in your mind.

How about taking the whole discourse up another octave? Use the word "opportunity." This is a great word. It denotes some kind of advantage or a combination of favorable circumstances. When you are looking at a set of lousy energies heading your way, say, "I am faced with an unexpected opportunity." Within difficulties lies the creative opportunity to not just resolve the problem but actually improve the situation. There is a lesson, a victory, a new way. Focus attention on finding these, and you will lead a more prosperous life.

When you are confronted with challenges, right before you brush your teeth, stand at your mirror and say, "I like myself," "I am the best," and "I can do it." Create positive affirmations that make sense to your life situation. Say these fifty times a day—more if you want to. Say them out loud so you can actually hear them. Smile to yourself as you do this exercise. Sure, you might feel funny at first. Who cares? You have created sludge in your mind and have to cleanse and drain it of the negativity. You have heard of people that go through fasting or other ways to clear out bodily toxins. Your mind is no different. You have to clear out the toxins here, too. Drive new, positive energy into your subconscious and reprogram your mind.

When you train your mind with positive self-talk, and when you keep your words and visualizations focused on your goals, you build success patterns. Be determined! Nothing will ever stop you from becoming your very best.

How about this self-talk? "I shouldn't have spoken up in that meeting and contradicted my boss. I'm hopeless when it comes to playing the game and buying into organizational politics. My job stresses me out and undermines my self-control. I'll never get to be a division manager; I ought to just say I'm a loser and that's it."

Don't we all sometimes come across not as well as we intended, or say something we wished we could rephrase? This kind of negative self-talk is depressing. How about if we replay the inner dialogue with a different, more positive angle? "I wish I had started my statement with an affirmation instead of critique. I'm smart enough to know not to do this. Looking back, I realize I just wanted to impress people with my detailed knowledge of the project. I just need to calm down, listen effectively, and add thoughts when appropriate. People will recognize my insight. Mistakes are just part of the learning process of business life."

Which of the above will provide more healthy self-esteem and long-term motivation? Our self-talk creates our emotional state and how we feel about ourselves. You have the power to develop yourself; you have the potential. Programming occurs early on in life by receiving and then repeating messages from significant others. We received many messages while growing up during our formative years. It's up to us, as adults, to accept the fact that we are now responsible for injecting ourselves with new, powerful, and positive messaging. Yes, we may have received negative messages when growing up, but now realize you have the power to change. Reprogram yourself to be more successful. Give yourself new messages that program you to win. Change the program, change your thinking. The more positive affirmations you make, the more you change your future.

"Shoulds," "oughts," "musts" . . . these absolute terms do much to evoke guilt. When you say, "I'm fifty—I should have made it to a vice president by now," it hurts your self-esteem. We distort reality when we think in extremes. Life is usually not in absolutes. Try not to overgeneralize or take an example or occasion and blow it out of proportion.

Our challenge is to acknowledge our psychological state to ourselves, and then see the power of optimism. Take our above example of job loss. Instead of saying to yourself you're a loser or that it's hopeless, try saying: "I wish I hadn't been laid off. But I know I bring a lot to the table in my field of expertise. By being forced out of my comfort zone, I have a unique opportunity to grow and develop new skills with a new maturity in life. It's my goal to turn this crisis into opportunity and make even better things happen to me in life."

Through positive self-talk, you begin to shape your psyche and put into place a positive energy. When you see things positively, you become a positive person—it's that simple. A job layoff is a situation that offers opportunity, not a problem.

If you are a small business owner, you are going to go through some tough times. It's challenging to be captain of your own ship, but that is the choice you made when you decided to be independent. When times are tough, and they will be, take solace in the fact you have freedom. You don't have to go to meetings and play politics. You don't have to be subservient to your boss or be nonassertive.

Positive thinking is validated by a recent new type of psychology that studies strengths and virtues that help make a person happy, productive, and excited about the future. *Positive psychology* wants to make everybody's life better and happier. Martin Seligman of the University of Pennsylvania is best known for this recent work. One could argue that the humanistic psychologists of the 1950s and 1960s laid the foundation for this movement. Psychologists such as Abraham Maslow and Carl Rogers discussed authenticity, self-discovery, and peak experiences.

Seligman describes positive psychology as "the scientific study of the strengths and virtues that enable individuals and communities to thrive." People, according to this new branch of psychology, want to live lives with meaning. They want to develop their strengths and live life to the fullest. Reflecting on your past and coming to terms with it, being happy in the here and now, and having an optimistic view of the future are the pillars of the movement.

Instead of viewing the darker and destructive aspects of the psyche as Freud did, they look at the higher-order, higher self of what mankind is, such as caring about others more than oneself; loving completely, not just to receive love; honesty and being true to who your ideal self is; courage to overcome adversity; compassion for your fellow human; and coming back from being defeated. From being down and out, and rising again, one becomes wiser. Being an ethical and responsible leader who is tolerant and promotes teamwork is more in line with how they think of leadership.

Psychology has shown that the continual use of a thought process begins the power of actualization. When you continuously think certain thoughts, eventually your behavior reflects these thoughts. Positive behavior results when we constantly put positive messages into our psyches. This has been written about and shown to be true throughout the ages.

8

Becoming Your Vision

Business is as varied and evolving as the human condition. New types of businesses are being created, as well as different means of conducting business. These new approaches will eventually be revealed. Who knows what forms of goods and commerce will be manufactured and traded a hundred years from now? For example, as this is being written, the emerging technologies of solar, wind, biofuel, and batteries will play an important role in our energy usage over the next generation. All these new businesses are in a potential state until executives with their conscious desires make the connection between what is potential and what is concrete. The successful company is the connecting filament between the possible business and the actual physical manifestation of the business.

> An idea, to be suggestive, must come to the individual with the force of a revelation.
>
> —William James

Albert Einstein postulated the theory of relativity. The energies that made his remarkable theory possible were already present. His genius was the connecting filament that revealed the underlying principles.

A far simpler business example that illustrates the point is a Mexican restaurant close to our office. The minute the restaurant opened, the place was packed, and it's been packed ever since. There was a hidden demand for quality Mexican food in the surrounding community. Those restaurateurs had the foresight to make the restaurant a reality. The restaurateurs were the filament between the potential and the concrete manifestation of that eatery.

In this abstract sense, you never *create* a new business; you *reveal* it. The underlying energy for success is already there. This is the heart of the entrepreneurial company—asking the right questions. "What opportunity are people overlooking that we could uncover and reveal? What's the connection between two apparently different concepts? What is it people want and are willing to pay for that they're not getting?" When you ask these questions, you try to spotlight the hidden potential for commercialism.

Your vision for your own career or for driving your department to greater innovation, or for opening your own company, doesn't magically spring into awareness. There's a seed that grows. The initial idea dances at the fringes of consciousness. Thoughts are kicked around in your head but outside direct awareness. Yet enough of the idea leaks through and nags to be articulated. Often, the nucleus of the idea comes to you in various forms. The idea begins to reverberate. The goal becomes clearer and clearer. It's revealed in a sudden "Aha!"—usually in your morning shower. The idea grows and gains even more weight as the angles of the idea come into awareness. Eventually, the idea is brought into concrete reality through hard work and focused effort. You're like a sculptor turning primitive granite into a beautiful chiseled form.

Within the initial kernel of your dream lies the potential for your whole career or vision for your organization, even if you initially don't know this. The vision's potential is dim at first. An analogy is a seed that contains the capacity to grow into a mighty redwood. Inside that seed of an idea is the true opportunity. Essentially, the seed is the germinating foundation, the fundamental concept upon which the tree of business is built. If the seed contains flaws, that tree will never be healthy and substantial unless true changes are made in the DNA of the idea.

➔ What is your seed of an idea?

Do you have an idea that dances at the fringe of your consciousness? Concentrate and bring it out!

ENVISIONING YOUR DREAM

The basics of visualization are easy. Begin by relaxing. Sit or lie in a comfortable position. Allow each part of your body to relax, starting at your toes and channeling relaxing energy up to your head. As you do this, take slow, deep breaths. This should take a few minutes.

The second step is to visualize the successful completion of your goal. Try to imagine what your office will look like. Picture yourself giving a presentation to a group of senior executives that are smiling and nodding as you review your idea. Imagine yourself leading a group of your employees in how they can move the company ahead. Envision yourself at the head of a long boardroom table with your team around you in rapt attention as you talk about how exciting the future is going to be and their roles in it.

Doing these practice runs helps you "see" and prepare for when it comes time to manifest your dream. Picture the idea precisely. See yourself as actually having achieved your goal. Constantly keep this picture in your mind throughout the day, while you're driving, while you're making dinner, and so on. Keep reviewing the picture, over and over, implanting it deeply in your subconscious and your conscious awareness. Believe, with all your heart, that this visual image is real. It is up to you to bring it into concrete reality, but it already exists and the universe wants you to have it. You will make it happen.

Take two minutes to do the above mental exercise—imagine your vision coming into physical reality.

When we visualize in our mind's eye, we tap into our unlimited mind. Your goal in visualizing is to connect to all the possibilities and creative solutions. Be open to an unexpected, wild idea. Develop a constructive skepticism. Challenge the status quo, the accepted wisdom of business colleagues, society, and even yourself. The skepticism is directed to things people think you can't do. Take the opposite road. Be skeptical of what you have been taught about the limits of your training and the limits set on you by well-meaning others.

This is hard. We are conditioned to think conservatively. We don't even know it. For example, when a certain idea is repeated at conferences, written about in publications, and shown on TV, it eventually works its way into the consciousness of people. If enough CEOs think we're headed into a recession, we are.

When the top 20 percent of the upper-income bracket starts believing an idea as accepted truth, it forms reality. Visionary executives don't automatically accept the usual dogma and prevailing opinion. Instead, they ask themselves questions that can't be easily answered. Take the story of Christopher Columbus. The small minds knew he'd sail off the end of the world, didn't they? Now, there was a great executive! He had a concept that was distinctive, got his idea funded by venture capital, and set sail— and the rest is history.

The trick to unleashing your vision is not being too rational when you contemplate your ideas. Allow yourself to be a child.

Children have a marvelous ability to role-play and imagine themselves as all kinds of characters—pirates, Wonder Woman, cops and robbers—and they get totally engrossed in the vision. A successful leader needs this childlike quality of believing in the metaphysical realm to imagine herself as wonderfully successful, to project herself through her imagination into triumph. Don't superimpose restrictions or doubt on your visualizing. Once you break free of your purely rational consciousness, you'll see a different type of reality, a reality that is more open, free, and evolving—one that places you in a position of control and power over your environment.

People intuitively know their own truths. You know what you know. But the rational mind wants more analysis. At the end of the day, additional facts merely confirm what you thought. Second-guessing makes people anxious and hurts confidence. If you let your purely rational mind visualize, it immediately starts setting constraints, limits, shoulds, and oughts. You need to break free of those constraints. You don't need drugs or alcohol; you only need to not allow your ego to constrain you. Close your eyes, become relaxed, and say to yourself that you're not going to allow any negative thinking, any limits. If you want to be a musician, visualize yourself as gloriously successful as the Beatles. If you dream of being president of a division, let your mind read the press release that appeared in your local paper heralding the town's newest "somebody." If you want to open up your own architectural firm, see yourself sitting down with superwealthy people and designing a unique vision—think of Frank Lloyd Wright's Falling Water, only better.

Right now, close your eyes again and visualize what you ultimately want in life. Don't allow any negative thoughts or limits of any kind!

> *Imagination is more important than knowledge.*
> —Albert Einstein

Go to any kindergarten class. You'll see children with a sense of wonder, inquisitiveness, and a need for self-expression, often developed through art. These core instincts are primal imperatives to unlock one's highest potential. As we have all experienced, these core instincts erode and fade. Parents, friends, society, and the corporate world beat our dreams out of us. As we mature, we become "realistic." We forget how to build castles. Becoming a top executive or opening your own company is your chance to regain what is rightfully yours. It gives you the chance to develop a deep level of desire that you still have, the ability to dream and visualize. Imagine your work helping to unfold yourself to your highest attributes. This is your genetic heritage.

Throughout your life, you've observed people who are intelligent, educated, and experienced but are working for other people who take risks. Why? Essentially, many bright people lose their childlike qualities of believing in magic, of believing they can fly or transform. They become adults. Their beliefs grow up, too. They no longer believe in fairy tales or miracles. If you can't believe in your dream, then you can't visualize yourself in the role of a successful leader. Don't let this happen to you—it's all right to dream like a child, no matter how old you are.

> *The secret of genius is to carry the spirit of the child into old age, which means never losing your enthusiasm.*
> —Aldous Huxley

BELIEVING IS SEEING

The usual axiom we're told as children is "Seeing is believing." In other words, your rational mind needs, and must have, actual proof before you believe something. From this perspective, unless there is left-brain validation through one of the five senses, something doesn't or can't exist. But the successful leader knows differently, even though he might not be able to verbalize or even be aware of it. He recognizes that the opposite is true—"Believing is seeing"—because of the gift of being able to visualize what he wants in his mind's eye. He'll eventually employ the (perhaps) intellectually brighter person who sticks with "Seeing is believing." We are advocating transcending pure logic and rationality so the world of possibilities opens wide. The literal rational mind has difficulty making the conceptual leap in the imagination to see opportunities in the marketplace. Desire with your heart, not simply with your brain.

Thoughts are a form of reality. They produce success in your life. Anyone who doubts thinking or believing will form into three-dimensional reality need only analyze the stories of people who heal themselves through the power of beliefs. Healing is known to occur from the placebo effect: Given only a sugar pill, a person who believes she is receiving medication often gets better. Their belief causes physiological changes.

The mind can control matter. Visualization happens first. Then, with sustained concentration, the image is brought into concrete reality. This is genetically hard-wired into our psyches. We've literally forgotten this metaphysical truism. Have you ever seen a golfer hit a shot and then contort his body in the direction he wishes the ball to go? Or when a person putts, then tries to guide the golf ball with her eyes to the hole? They're both tapping into a deep concept without knowing it—our minds create the reality we experience. The ball doesn't change its trajectory when we twist, but this unconscious action demonstrates and reveals our deepest conditioning. We might laugh when we catch ourselves doing this next time on the links, but we'll keep doing it—we literally can't help it. Why? Because it's true. Our thoughts *do* create our reality. Our spontaneous actions reveal our deepest conditioning.

People who accept this know how to program their minds with success. Sure enough, the success eventually manifests itself. Science teaches that observation of something is needed before it becomes reality. It's impossible to separate our observation from the physical manifestation of the object in question. When your vision is constant and grounded and you see it in its entirety, it's only a matter of time before it's brought into the physical realm. Once you acknowledge and accept this, confidence soars in whatever it is you are trying to create, from your own firm to the boardroom. You don't *believe* you can do it; you *know* it. And knowing something gives you more confidence than just believing something.

Your vision must exist before the means to achieve it comes into existence. In other words, when you contemplate an idea initially, try to see the end result, not the means of getting there. The more fully you can develop, define, and articulate the end vision, the better your chances for success. Even in that potential state, there must be a completion of the creative process in advance. Constantly look at the larger picture. Don't get dragged down into details. The entire process first manifests in your mind. It is important to not jump into the details too quickly. Take the time to visualize your dream in its entirety.

But thinking big also means caring about the little aspects. When you take care of the little things, you take care of the big things—when you care about a penny, you'll make millions. You don't have to take care of the details personally, but you need to find somebody who does. Some people think big but do not do the necessary work of taking care of all the details that turn the vision into reality. Recognize that "the devil is in the details." When you take care of the details, you stay out of trouble.

> → Reflect on this question frequently: Does my present activity relate to the vision?

DON'T LET YOUR EGO GET IN YOUR WAY

We're proponents of education, both formal or informal—especially the concept of viewing life as a long educational experience. The guy who drops out of high school or college limits himself in most senses. But the dropout, once he gets older and takes life seriously, might be willing to do things a more educated person won't. The person with less pride doesn't let self-importance get in his way and hold him back.

For example, one client who was a highly successful entrepreneur owned a company that repaired automobile brakes and installed mufflers. He built his business up to forty-five stores, lived in a beautiful home, and was known and respected in the business community. When he began his business in his late twenties, he stood out in front of his first store with a sign and waved people in as they drove by. Would a guy with an MBA from a top school get dressed up in a costume and make enough of a spectacle so people would remember the service and be intrigued enough to bring their car in? Probably not. But this tenth-grade dropout eventually had some awfully smart MBAs working for him!

The point is, just because you're smart and highly educated doesn't mean you can't have fun and imagine. It seems that the more formal education you receive, the more left-brained you become. Don't let education destroy your ability to dream.

Sometimes being a bit of a character helps, because you have to live up to your own persona. When you're memorable because of your appearance or behavior, you can sometimes get up above the noise of similar businesses or services. Great leaders tend to be individualists, not rebels. Many people who are rebellious have ego or self-image problems. Their behavior doesn't so much reflect independence or individualism as much as a need to be noticed and acknowledged. Rebellious people justify their behavior to themselves, never realizing the deeper reasons for their antics: the need to be validated.

DREAM BIG

Imagine a landscape. In that landscape exists the past, present, and future of your career. Imagine yourself looking back and having done the things necessary to make it successful. Executives have dreams and hopes but are not clairvoyant. You can't predict where your career might take you—the twists and turns, mergers and acquisitions, that might ultimately happen. But all of us have the power to imagine our future and to paint that future with any colors and shapes we desire. Visualize what the ultimate manifestation can be. Your dreams are limited only by desire. Reflect upon your vision not as a prayer or hope, but as a reality that wants to be brought into concrete substance. In your mind's eye, make the dream complete. Imagine things in their finest detail—walking into the lobby for the first time, what your office will look like, putting your key in your own door.

Believe in your abilities to take yourself to this level. This belief is the only way creative juices keep flowing and the necessary energy keeps pouring into your physiological and psychological system. People sell themselves short. They don't dare dream and visualize what they can become. They don't think they're worthy, smart, or talented enough. But they're wrong. They are valuable enough to contribute to society and themselves by being a successful business leader. Don't be one of the millions who sell themselves short.

Close your eyes right now and visualize your idea in its highest potential form. See it in your mind's eye, and feel it taking form. Think about the details. All parts must come together to realize the whole.

SUSTAINING YOUR VISION

Ultimately, you'll sustain your motivation and excitement if your career has a self-actualizing quality to it. In other words, when your career is more than a way of making a dollar, it creates a long-term vision and helps you and your employees' internal motivation. When you see your career as something important to society, you'll take pride in what you do. Your career ideally taps into your highest level of creativity and reasons for your existence.

If you wrote down the five things you most want out of life, your list would undoubtedly take on some aspects of self-actualization. Sure, there would be the usual wishes concerning financial security and relationships. But eventually thoughts such as wisdom, peace of mind, deeply knowing yourself, or being able to contribute to the world through a responsible product or service would make the list.

→ What are the five most important things you want to have achieved before you pass on?

INTUITIVE EXECUTIVES

Complicated decisions cannot be dissected into all of their component factors. People are placed in high levels of responsibility because they accurately predict the outcome of events through seeing the subtleties of variables. Objective information such as facts and numbers is combined with subjective information—feelings. Look beyond what is seen and heard physically. There is a subtle energy you can intuit.

Intuition, like many higher-level concepts, stubbornly resists precise definition. From the Latin *intuire,* it literally means "looking within" or "regarding from within." But the process is totally contained within each person. We can describe the meaning of the word as it relates to us. Every person defines intuition differently. Intuition is the ability to feel the energy being projected by a situation—an immediate flash of awareness, understanding, and synthesis of the totality or wholeness of an event. Intuition points to possibilities.

Intuition is spontaneous. It seems to come without an active effort on the part of the person feeling it. Reasoning, on the other hand, is the process of accumulating facts and making deductions based on those facts—a process that takes place over time with deliberate and sustained effort.

Intuition:

- is the gestalt or unified pattern of your thought processes and internal perceptions—a leap in reasoning based on many bits of information, but which reaches a conclusion beyond and greater than all those bits.
- occurs when your thoughts are distilled into a focused whole that breaks through to your conscious awareness. In a state of contemplation, ideas pass through your mind. Suddenly there is a flash. When the flash ends, the intellect takes over to process and interpret what has just been revealed.
- already exists as a synthesis in our consciousness. With every thought, we contribute to this pool and provide a larger pool from which to draw. Through study, effort, and experience, we build a reservoir of knowledge that is used for higher levels of awareness. Perception isn't knowledge, and further, knowledge isn't wisdom. Neither knowing nor wisdom leads

to doing. It is only through acting on your intuition that you make the leap from information to wisdom.

- is visual. Visualization of ideas is the creative power of imagination plus focused mental energy. Use your mind's eye. Imagine a situation and visualize its every possible manifestation. Allow your intuition to work, developing it by picturing your situation vividly in all of its detail. Sense all of the intricacies, flavor, and vivid emotions. This isn't an academic approach which is overly intellectual and wants to be "right"—that misses the point. To intuit, you must focus on a bigger picture and not get mired in detail.

➔ When have you used your intuition successfully?

➔ When have you experienced an intuitive thought or idea you should have acted on?

➔ What was the consequence of not acting on your intuition?

BENEFITS OF INTUITION

- *Intuition is multidimensional.* Intuition allows you to be multidimensional. It would be great if you could whiteboard all the processes, points, boxes, and lines and then come to some kind of decision that takes all the variables into account. But do you have the 160 IQ or all year to figure it out? The truth is, you cannot know all the dynamics that comprise a situation. Through intuition, even if the situation is not fully understood, a good decision can be made.
- *Intuition is practical.* True intuition is always practical. Excellent business decisions are eminently practical. This is of primary importance. Intuition is a direct path, the line of least resistance. It is elegantly simple, yet accurate. In most circumstances, simplicity has the advantage over complexity. The truer something is, the faster it takes effect. Intuition provides an exact understanding of purpose and direction with a parsimonious expenditure of applied energy.
- *Intuition instills confidence.* Once you learn to look at a situation clearly and use intuition, you implement decisions with no regret or remorse—an inner calmness prevails. We second-guess ourselves when decisions are not in agreement with the wisdom of our intuition.
- *Intuition facilitates prediction.* People who are integrated and in touch with themselves have insights that are considered almost clairvoyant. Peaceful, mature people have common sense. They exhibit sound judgment and the ability to examine

several situations, see relationships and possible outcomes, and choose the correct path.

- *Intuition fosters creative thinking.* Creative thinking is a form of intuition. Creative people see analogies; they feel, sense, and see links. Their minds reveal associations between two apparently different and distinct concepts. Their perception is unique and reveals what the rational mind, using testimonial, inference, and deduction, cannot reveal. Their creativity is seeing combinations or realizing connections. Creativity is the skill and disposition you need to tap into your unconscious and bring ideas to awareness.

Creativity requires the courage to let go of certainties.
—Erich Fromm

ENHANCING INTUITION

I suggest that you have within you the ability to mentor yourself through your "higher self." As we have discussed, your higher self is that vision of yourself with all your potential realized. Most never get there, but that goal is the positive motivation. Never underestimate your higher self, expressed through intuition, gained through working and living. Gradual recognition and acceptance of the wisdom of your intuition is a signal of transformation to greater maturity—a critical link to your personal and professional growth. Inspiration (the "breathing in" of an idea from a higher influence) comes with a sincere interest in what you are doing.

Intuition is largely self-taught, recognized, and developed gradually. Your challenge is to consistently acknowledge your intuition. Recognize when it is speaking to you. Have enough self-confidence to believe and accept your intuition, and to take action. It generally takes many years of living before we learn to truly listen to ourselves. Some people learn to do so in high school and have great careers going by the time they are in their late twenties. Some never learn to trust their intuition. Don't be one of those.

Constraints and limitations are overcome through imagination. Judgment stifles creativity. Statements like "Let's be realistic," "That won't work here," "It has been tried before," "That's fine in theory, but . . .," "Our employees just won't change," or "My boss can't see a new and better way" block people from considering alternatives.

Intuition is subject to control and enhancement through the intellectual mind. Concentration focuses and reorients your energy. Random thoughts with a high dose of emotion need to be subjugated to your higher consciousness, which is focused. Concentration is intellectual, not emotional. When we are intellectual and able to concentrate, we focus more deeply and fully on the problem at hand. Top-performing executives invariably have the ability to concentrate.

Working from the assumption that everything is possible, imagine your job if it were ideal. Suspend criticism, evaluation, and judgment about the possibility of the ideal.

→ How much do you really enjoy your work?
→ What would have to happen for you to enjoy your work even more?
→ How would your job tasks be ideally performed?
→ What are the differences between the imagined ideal and the current state?

There are two essential questions in life: Who am I? and Who do I want to be?—the real self versus the ideal self.

→ What is holding you back from achieving your ideal self?

When everything you do is predictable, year-in and year-out, you become settled in your thoughts and reactions. Forget what you have done and start fresh. Become unsettled in your thinking. Being dynamic means to destroy. Be ever alert to the possibility of error and distortions; constantly try to keep an open mind. Imagination is reached by an informal and unstructured mode of reasoning. Listen to your "inner voice" with an open mind.

Most really good ideas do not occur to us on the job. Busy work environments do not foster calmness and tranquility. Great ideas come when you are at home, at rest, or pursuing a hobby or some activity that has nothing to do with the situation you were pondering. You feel relaxed, at peace, in harmony with yourself—and suddenly the intuitive insight manifests. We all had experiences like this. You are not thinking about the situation confounding you and the answer comes to you seemingly without effort. Our answers may not be in our conscious awareness. By asking the right question and relaxing the mind, we receive communication from our unconscious.

PREDICTING THE FUTURE

Intuition is the art of registering your responsiveness to phenomena. The clearer, the more sensitive, and the deeper your capacity to register your impressions, the more easily your higher consciousness speaks to you.

When you are going to meet a person for the first time, or when driving to a client's office for the first time, practice intuition by trying to visualize what the client will be like or what kind of office the client might have. Intuit what the customer is going to say. What kind of mood will he or she be in? Your goal is an increased ability to perceive the thoughts and feelings of others—this is a sign of increased intuition. You may not be correct, but your mental rehearsal will give you confidence and help you to be relaxed.

9

Becoming Your Core Competencies

"Business competency" is a term that describes the knowledge and skills of an executive. This chapter describes the twenty-one competencies we use in our work with executives. In our coaching process, after an initial interview followed by a half-day of assessment using various kinds of personality and management tests, the client and the coach examine these competencies and rank-order the top three and the bottom three.

Our coaching has two overall streams: getting the client to understand how she could mold her job creatively (1) to include more of her competency strengths, and (2) to work around or improve the weaker areas. Go through the list and rate yourself on a 1–7 scale, with 1 meaning you believe you possess very little of the skill and 7 meaning you think you possess this skill in spades, that you are outstanding.

Note that the competencies are broken into many small statements. Try underlining the ones you need to improve on and placing a star next to the ones you believe you do exceptionally well. Thus, you break down the competencies into refined small assertions.

1. *Vision:* Able to describe the ideal future as a realistic "stretch" to how things can be; share a genuine belief/excitement of how the future can fulfill values/hopes/dreams; describe the future direction in a way that will motivate sacrifice/effort; involve others in building a shared vision; build confidence that a vision is realistic and worth added effort; use words like "see," "picture," "dream," and "what if"; link vision to broad strategy and specific tactics.

   1   2   3   4   5   6   7

2. *Innovation:* Able to challenge past practices/procedures and give reasons for change; generate new solutions to existing problems; suggest changes/new procedures which will improve performance;

suspend critical judgment to remain open to new perspectives; offer new ideas/methods to deal with opportunities and problems; involve others who can contribute to the creative process; generate multiple solutions to the same problem for review.

> 1   2   3   4   5   6   7

3. *Problem Analysis and Solving:* Able to anticipate/solve problems not resolved through existing work systems/procedures; gain involvement of stakeholders/opinion leaders in problem solving; prepare a written definition of problem causes, outcomes, obstacles, sticking points, and desirable outcomes; identify alternative solutions, anticipate implementation problems, and offer the best choice; monitor effectiveness at each stage of solution and adjust efforts; use disappointments to redesign solutions.

> 1   2   3   4   5   6   7

4. *Decisiveness:* Able to make decisions/take action in a timely and confident manner; develop action plans quickly; use challenges to gather new information without minimizing action under way; monitor feedback to evaluate decisions/make adjustments; make needed decisions in the absence of complete information; stand by prior decisions until convinced otherwise; avoid second-guessing decisions; assume responsibility for decisions even if there are negative outcomes.

> 1   2   3   4   5   6   7

5. *Advocate Productive Change:* Able to support and implement productive change in the face of conflict/tension/risk; challenge standard ways of doing things and introduce new initiatives; advocate the change process through willing effort/spoken word; promote/champion change in spite of obstacles/resistance; question why things are done the way they are; resist change that may be unsafe/illegal/unethical; explain how new duties and roles relate to achieving a better future.

> 1   2   3   4   5   6   7

6. *Adapt to Change:* Able to learn new processes/policies/skills; listen with an open mind to plans for change; adopt new job tasks/priorities/work habits to replace past ways of doing things;

question the effectiveness of change to those in charge in a reasonable, informed manner; use physical activity/exercise to cope with the pressure/expectations associated with change; try out new ways of doing things in a sincere way; gain beneficial feedback from problems during change.

1	2	3	4	5	6	7

7. *Assertive Conviction:* Able to state a belief/opinion in a mature, factual manner; express opinions directly without abuse/anger/intimidation/manipulation/hasty compromise; hear the opinions/feelings of others and show listening by restatement/summary/paraphrasing; use tactful repetition to persistently offer ideas/feelings; stand up for rights/opinions; say no as needed; show confidence through eye contact/clear speech/body language; challenge authority/procedures/policy in a respectful way.

1	2	3	4	5	6	7

8. *Resilience:* Able to adapt to work pressure/deadlines/interpersonal tension/long hours in a calm, productive manner; recover quickly from setbacks; spring back even after failure/disappointments; use self-talk/deep breathing and monitor behavior to minimize stress; avoid emotional flare-ups and loud voice/sarcasm.

1	2	3	4	5	6	7

9. *Goal Setting:* Able to convert gaps between a current state and desires into specific, measurable, challenging, and realistic goals; write goals using language that describes what will be seen or heard when the goal is achieved; involve stakeholders in goal setting; recognize that challenging goals represent some risk of not being able to be achieved; acknowledge the effort and persistence required to reach outcome goals; convert complex goals into smaller learning objectives which are steps to a larger goal; identify the milestones/deadlines/red flags to measure goal progress.

1	2	3	4	5	6	7

10. *Organization and Planning:* Able to anticipate and arrange the resources needed to reach objectives; adopt a systematic approach for time management; use a calendar to schedule tasks/priorities/appointments/meetings; maintain a filing/data management system;

manage multiple details without losing overall perspective on the work to be done; adjust/develop/integrate plans with stakeholders; describe the priorities/time/sequence of steps to take; monitor goal progress; develop contingency plans to adapt to obstacles.

1   2   3   4   5   6   7

11. *Drive for Results:* Able to commit long hours and make sacrifices to get results; take personal responsibility for results; show a "can-do" approach to work; persist in the face of obstacles/constraints/ setbacks; put tasks/goals over socializing/personal interests; manage multiple tasks based on an understanding of priorities; compete against self to improve performance; assume manageable risk based on an ability to influence outcomes; communicate with words like "push," "excel," "goals," and "results"; give priority to work over personal life; independently do more than is expected/required.

1   2   3   4   5   6   7

12. *Self-Direction:* Able to work in a disciplined/self-directing way when not guided by supervision/policy/procedures; set goals/prioritize tasks/take reasonable action without being told to do so; generate high levels of work output without supervision; allocate reasonable time and resources needed to achieve tasks without waiting for permission; assume personal responsibility for success and failure; demonstrate commitment to excellence by monitoring performance; maintain tools/resources/ work environment without being reminded.

1   2   3   4   5   6   7

13. *Continuous Improvement:* Able to question how to improve processes/systems/methods to increase reliability/quality/efficiency of work; look for gaps between how things are and how things can be; question if the correct goals are being pursued; seek new learning which will introduce ways to improve work skills; encourage others to provide ideas/suggestions for improvement; distinguish between individual performance and systems performance; use written work standards to develop measures and improve performance.

1   2   3   4   5   6   7

14. *Teamwork and Collaboration:* Able to support cooperative work relationships by adapting interests and preferences to team needs; recognize the difference between team priorities and personal wants; build mutual trust/respect/cooperation with team members; conform to agreed ways to work together; contribute to the team with ideas/suggestions/effort; participate in team meetings actively; avoid talking about team members negatively in their absence; share information important to the team's work; support team decisions once made; learn from team mistakes.

1   2   3   4   5   6   7

15. *Influence and Persuasion:* Able to persuade others to take action/accept an idea or change; ask questions to identify possible points of influence; use tactful, persistent repetition to present a point of view; adapt efforts to persuade in light of the situation/objections/resistance; make a dramatic statement to gain attention and persuade; offer compelling information/evidence to support an idea/change; cede secondary issues in order to maximize influence on primary issues; earn trust by being honest/credible; reinforce decisions/changes by encouragement and reassurance.

1   2   3   4   5   6   7

16. *Leadership:* Able to influence others to take effective action to reach goals; adapt leadership style to the situation by being either more participative or directive; communicate in a way that builds credibility/respect/motivation/recognition/high performance; ask team members for opinions and give time for discussion; maintain objectivity and procedures needed to create a stable understanding of how to get things done; promote cooperation between teams; use performance problems as training opportunities; reward high performance; create events to celebrate team success; talk regularly with people who resist new directions/ideas.

1   2   3   4   5   6   7

17. *Coaching and Developing:* Able to draw upon past experiences to support self-discovery and personal growth; make time to listen and respond to the client's agenda; use a systematic approach to define/achieve developmental objectives; ask questions to

understand feelings around development; gain agreement on actions to take; arrange for work situations to stretch and teach; explain how to self-monitor; provide constructive performance feedback to reinforce new learning; explain important business values; develop job assignments which will help the client grow/get promotions; be an example of organizational citizenship.

1　　2　　3　　4　　5　　6　　7

18. *Energize Others:* Able to show energy/motivation to do work well; speak in a way that reflects confidence and enthusiasm; be an example of smiling and positive gestures; describe how things can be because of productive attitudes and effort; talk about goal setting as a tool for self-motivation; give respect regardless of status; talk about success stories/positive role models as examples to follow; encourage others to make positive motivation show in their work; identify the important values/rewards/motivators of followers; use personal issues/loyalties to motivate performance.

1　　2　　3　　4　　5　　6　　7

19. *Organizational Savvy:* Able to use organizational dynamics/values/politics to get work done; build and maintain partnerships and alliances to build support/share information; identify trusted sources of "underground"/"insider" information; volunteer information to trusted colleagues even when it creates political risk; protect confidences/sources of information; test rumors with trusted coworkers; share information on how to get things done effectively; work around organizational silos/roadblocks which interfere with gaining results; predict how personal likes/dislikes will influence decisions; anticipate the impact of changes on individuals/work groups/programs.

1　　2　　3　　4　　5　　6　　7

20. *Relationship Management:* Able to develop/maintain high rapport/warm relationships; take time needed to offer respectful, undivided attention to a person; smile/use open gestures/be positive to put people at ease; ask questions to show interest/concern/helpfulness; express opinions directly/clearly without abuse or manipulation; state opinions on sensitive topics tactfully; create a reliable flow of honest information; raise issues and work through

relationship problems; ask for feedback regarding what was said; maintain professional language/conduct during conversations; avoid and discourage gossip/negative comments/hearsay; get out of a comfort zone to be on another person's terms.

1   2   3   4   5   6   7

21. *Meeting Leadership:* Able to conduct introductions/seminars/ presentations in a way that makes points clearly; use a purposeful, time-efficient approach to managing a presentation; adopt body language/gestures which support the ideas being presented; prepare presentations thoroughly to be clear; encourage participation by asking questions of the audience; keep the presentation on time and on topic by tactfully redirecting the conversation.

1   2   3   4   5   6   7

→ From your responses above, which are your top three? How can you more effectively incorporate these competencies into your job/career?

→ What are your bottom three competencies? How can you creatively compensate for or improve them enough so they aren't detrimental?

10

Summary

Long before you read *Becoming Your Own Business Coach*, you were aware of factors that caused you not to be as successful as you wished for in life. And, of course, we aren't necessarily talking about just careers, although that certainly is the focus here. Each of us has some type of addiction or life issue that stumps us. We try to control and contain it as best we can, and we are generally fairly successful. Sure, we lapse and fail in our own eyes. But we also succeed a lot of the time, too. You hold down a good job, you come to work on time, you have friends and family, and you have formed and lived positive values. These achievements should be acknowledged about yourself, to yourself. You are also aware of some strengths that have caused success. The question is, through this book and subsequent self-analysis, will you move forward at an accelerated level? That is the goal: acceleration beyond what life would have done for you anyway.

Regard *Becoming Your Own Business Coach* as a book that, hopefully, helped you grow. Yet the book is only a single source of reference. Executive growth is continuous, because all of it is the acquisition of wisdom. I say this with humor because, in its raw state, this is what life is all about. To lead or own your own business is a privilege. The best way you can reward your employees is for you to be a wise leader.

Remember that you will develop yourself strongly and resolutely as you say "I can" and "I will." This endeavor is no different than anything else that takes willpower and a sense of purpose.

It is really a personal matter, based on your own philosophy of life, how far you wish to take your executive development. At the more senior levels, there is no difference between executive development and personal development. At some point, you might feel satisfied that you are OK where you're at and don't need any further development other than what life and the job offer in terms of aging and experience. But there are some who have a fundamental need to continue to evolve. They have a constructive dissatisfaction with themselves that pushes them to continually understand themselves and grow.

→ How satisfied are you right now with your level of psychological development?

Recognize that there is no such thing as being "finished" with growth as a person or an executive. Would you even *want* to have arrived at a place with no further step left to be taken? If you reflect on it, the answer is undoubtedly *no*. Life is all about the struggle and the effort to find happiness. The journey itself is the goal.

Thanks for reading *Becoming Your Own Business Coach.* I have tried through these words to share what I've learned over my career as a talent management consultant. Growth and change begin when you, through introspection and personal reflection, decide that you want to develop yourself as a leader or entrepreneur. Growth occurs when you see your ideal self as your mentor and challenge yourself to constantly evolve. Never quit or give in. Remain optimistic. Stay with your strengths. Remember to help others on their road to success and happiness. Be grateful for what you have.

I look forward to someday meeting you and listening to your stories of endeavor. Visualize your future and never stop dreaming. The world needs you to be successful!

Index

About the Author

GEORGE W. WATTS, ED.D., is a behavioral scientist, management consultant, and noted authority on leadership development. Dr. Watts rose to become a CEO in a public company, and was also an EVP of two mid-size firms. He has led talent management firms for many years. He has interviewed, assessed, and trained over five thousand "C" suite executives. For many years, he was the host of the popular Chicago-based radio program, *The Business Doctor*. Several years ago, he started his current talent management firm, AST Management in Chicago. Watts graduated from William and Mary College with a doctorate in counseling psychology. He is the author of *Power Vision* (Business One/Irwin, 1995) and has published numerous articles in professional journals. He is also a member of the Chicago Economic Club and currently a board member of the Society of Psychologists in Management. He is located in Chicago, Illinois. Check out his website www.DrGeorgeWatts.com to learn more about his firm.